2% CHANCE TO LIVE

FROM TRAGEDY TO TRIUMPH

JOHN GALINETTI

2% CHANCE TO LIVE
FROM TRAGEDY TO TRIUMPH

JOHN GALINETTI

© 2018 John Galinetti

Printed in the United States of America

ISBN-13: 978-0999629000

CONTENTS

ENDORSEMENTS

"With God, 2% is more than enough, and John's story is a modern-day miracle that anyone who is facing the biggest challenge in their lives needs to read. For with God, all things are possible...from the depths of hell to healing in 24 hours!" ~ **Harry and Cheryl Salem, Salem Family Ministries**

"What I know for sure — miracles happen and God is always present. After more than 20 years of caring for surgical and critical patients — miracles happen. Many hesitate or are reluctant to admit it. I have personally seen patients survive injuries and diseases that defy medicine and surgery. Pastor John's recovery was a miracle. Expected survival ... 2% was generous. As a surgeon it is unexplainable, but as a man of faith his recovery is easily explainable, a miracle. Pastor John is a great man of faith, my spiritual mentor and on fire for God. His work spreading the Gospel isn't finished so God intervened and John's miracle message was born." ~ **John Vance D.O. / FACS**

"I have seen the medical world do amazing things. It's wonderful when you can use medical science to prove God's existence ... In light of the fact that Pastor John was underwater for approximately 6-12 minutes the prognosis was grave. His chance of survival was probably less than 2%. Water filled his lungs and of course we were concerned that his brain had been compromised. In cases like these, you prepare the family for the inevitable. The outcome, instead, was nothing short of a miracle. What I witnessed in this case was proof that God is the ultimate physician."

~ Robert Bouvier, MD - attending physician

"From trauma to triumph, John Galinetti's life-altering record of events presented Life Preserving Principles everybody should use to overcome adversity. 2% Chance to Live is a 100% MUST READ!"

~ Chris Swanson, best-selling author, Tinman to IRONMAN, author of Blood, Guts and Things That Drive You Nuts. National inspirational speaker, founder of Swanson Leadership

"'Jesus Christ is the same yesterday and today and forever' is confirmed and made alive once again as you read the incredible account of Jesus' miraculous intervention in John's supernatural healing and recovery." **~ John W. Gunn, Founder and Executive Director of The Power Company Kids Club**

"John's story is breathtaking ... and 100% true. I've known John for over forty years and have never seen him waver from his strong faith. But a dramatic and tragic event left John struggling for his life, and only a miracle from God could rescue him. If you or someone you know is facing a physical or emotional battle, get this book, and learn how you too can beat the odds." ~ **Dr. Dave Williams, best-selling author and founder of Dave Williams Ministries**

"Pastor John's contagious passion, joy and faith come through the pages of this book. His story is a living testament to the reliability of God's promises, the impossible life He invites us into and how He ultimately works to make our greatest trials a platform to help others" ~ **Dominic Russo, founder of Missions. Me, 1Nation1Day**

"John Galinetti is the real deal ... a modern day 'Messenger of Christ' .... whose passion for life and saving souls is no less than 100%. Thought-provoking, inspiring and motivational! John's journey to death's door reminds us all that a 2% chance of living is a wake-up call for where we'll spend the other 98%. 2% is an adrenalizing ride through our fears and our faith! Throttling us through adversity with an overwhelming realization that God is always in control." ~ **Mike MacDonald, radio personality and cohost of "Mike & Stephanie in the Morning" on Flint's CK 105.5**

"What a joy and encouragement it was to read John Galinetti's gripping book, 2% Chance to Live. I was speaking at the conference the afternoon John's accident occurred, and I led a seminar and spoke at his church the Saturday and Sunday afterwards. Of course, the people of the church were concerned, but they had been taught the very principles that John expands upon in his book, and as a result, the people immediately responded with powerful faith. John and Wendy, through their obedience and pastoral leadership, had helped to raise up a church family that was able to lift them up in their most challenging hour. This is not just a book about trial and challenge; this is a book about triumph and conquest. I am confident it will inspire faith and hope in everyone who reads it." ~ **Tony Cooke, author, speaker and founder of Tony Cooke Ministries**

"From a horrible jet-ski accident, leaving him a 2% chance to live, to now a walking miracle. This book not only tells a dynamic story of faith and of God's healing power, but it also provides life principles on how to trust God and live by faith. Everyone can benefit from reading this amazing and inspirational true story. Pastor John's miracle story will build faith and challenge the reader to know that with God, all things are possible." ~ **Dr. Matthew T. Mangan, Pastor of Mount Hope Church Williamston, MI**

"John Galinetti's book could have been called, Yea Though I Walk Through the Valley of the Shadow of Death, I Will Fear No Evil, and taken its title from a wonderful verse that many of us learned during childhood. For John Galinetti though, that verse became a reality in a matter of seconds. The story of an accident which left him with a 2% chance to live, to now a walking miracle is a must read for every person facing a physical battle. Faith is real and still works today." ~ **Joe McGee, author, Bible teacher and former school administrator, and founder of Joe McGee Ministries and Faith for Families seminars**

FOREWORD

When I read the manuscript for *2% Chance to Live* I was moved with tears of joy and gratitude for God's unending grace. In the deepest times of tragedy, God really wants to dispatch a miracle to you, as he did for John.

This throbbing, fast-paced message is more than just an account of John's testimony. It's a guide for your life and a map for your future. In this book, John carefully demonstrates eight life-preserving principles each of us would do well to deposit into our hearts and minds. These principles could be instrumental in seizing your own miracle when facing a personal crisis.

I've known John Galinetti for over 35 years. John and his wife, Wendy, were both launched into full-time ministry as our first church planters. John and Wendy both felt the Holy Spirit calling them to Grand Blanc, so we sent them off with just a handful of people, an offering, and faith and excitement in their hearts. And it was through *that* faith along with unimaginable tenacity they established an influential, disciple-making, internationally recognized church and center for leadership training.

This book is about the mountain-moving strength of genuine faith. It's about the Holy Spirit's power to turn every dreadful situation into a God-made miracle. I remember getting that awful call. I had left John's leadership conference a little early that day because of other ministry meetings I had scheduled that week. When I received the call about John's accident, my heart sunk at first. Immediately I called my wife, our global prayer center director, to enlist scores of intercessors to unite on John's behalf. Faith started rising as our Spirit-filled prayer partners reported back with prophetic words of faith, confidence, and healing. I later learned that not only were our prayer partners activated, but intercessors from all over the nation and other parts of the world joined in to plead for John's miracle.

One of John's life-preserving biblical principles is this: "There is no distance in prayer." When I realized how many thousands of people, near and far, pulled together on behalf of John, I literally wept for joy, thanking God for His amazing Church on this earth.

Prepare now to be propelled into a faith venture that could save your life as you read *2% Chance to Live: From Tragedy to Triumph.* My prayer for you is that the Holy Spirit will repeatedly bring to your remembrance the eight life-preserving principles John used during his dark experience. These biblical principles have the power to turn a test into a testimony; a tragedy into a triumph!

Dr. Dave Williams
Dave Williams Ministries
Bishop, Mount Hope Church

PROLOGUE

The questions ran through my wife Wendy's mind like freight cars crashing into each other.

Was John going to survive? Would his lungs recover? How about his heart? And if he did make it, would he be brain dead?

She walked toward the entrance of Genesys Regional Medical Center in Grand Blanc, Michigan, on Saturday morning, the day after my bad accident. Still numb from the past eighteen hours — I had been dragged from the lake and taken to the hospital the previous afternoon — she was about to get a glimpse of her future when she walked into my ICU room. But nobody knew what it held. What shape would I be in? Would I be conscious? Would my lungs be functioning or failing? Would my body be getting enough oxygen to support life? When would I wake up, if ever?

Most pressing of all, if I regained consciousness, what kind of mind would I have left? I had been under water for anywhere from six to twelve minutes. I guess that's the reason I was given just a two percent chance to live.

That usually spells a death sentence or significant brain damage.

What kind of future am I looking at? Wendy couldn't help wondering. *What if John doesn't come back the way he was? What if he gets worse and doesn't make it through at all?*

In that moment, for the hundredth time, she stopped her mind from racing.

No, I'm not going there, she told herself with conviction. *God, I trust you fully with our future. I won't allow myself to imagine the worst. Whatever you have for us, I know you will be enough. I believe John will be fully healed and restored. Thank you for his complete recovery!*

She wasn't praying alone. Dozens, even hundreds of people in Grand Blanc, greater Michigan, Florida, California and elsewhere were sending up a united concert of prayer, bombarding heaven with the same request: *God, please save John's life!*

At that moment, the prospects, naturally speaking, seemed grim. Still, Wendy felt renewed peace as she stepped into the cool confines of the hospital and boarded the elevator to the fourth floor ICU. She was about to see what her future looked like.

CHAPTER 1

"How are you enjoying attending your own conference?" my friend, Pastor Dave Williams, asked in the lobby of the Holiday Inn event center. He slapped me on the arm with affection.

"More than you can imagine," I replied with a laugh. Pastor Dave was in town speaking at one of Mount Hope Church Grand Blanc's big events, held at a local hotel. For this conference, I was more relaxed than usual.

"I still wish you were speaking," Dave said. "I'd love to hear what you've been learning lately."

"Next time," I promised. "I feel so encouraged just taking part as a participant. You should try it sometime."

Usually, at our conferences, I was front and center much of the time, hosting, speaking, greeting, and making sure things ran correctly. Mount Hope Church, in Grand Blanc, is known for high-level gatherings that address critical topics like effective leadership, good marriages, outreach, cutting-edge ministry methods and more. Our goal is to train people to live and serve with greater excellence.

This time, I had decided to unplug and enjoy the conference as a participant. In more than twenty years as pastor of this church, I had learned that every leader needs to take time to receive, to recognize his limits. Plus, we had brought in two great speakers — Tony Cooke and Dave Williams. All week long the morning and evening sessions had been awesome, and the break-out sessions were just what people were looking for. Participants were building relationships and a sense of community with each other. It was a marvelous thing to see. I found myself basking in moments of relaxation and inspiration, getting filled with new energy and ideas as the outstanding speakers shared wisdom and insight.

Thank you, Lord, for such a great week, I prayed as I said good-bye to Dave and made my way to the morning session. I had another thing to be grateful for as I breathed that prayer. That afternoon, I planned to slip away and get one last jet ski ride in before winter. September was here and it was just about time to put the jet skis away until spring. My destination would be Lake Fenton, a short drive from our house. All week long I had pictured myself cutting and jetting around the lake on my Sea

Doo XP Limited, as I loved to do. The XP Limited was an amazing machine, built for darting and breathtaking speed. They called it a white-knuckle machine. It had a huge amount of torque which translated into raw power on the water. When I pulled back on the throttle I felt like I was riding an uncaged lion.

It'll be the perfect end to the perfect week, I thought as I sat down and got ready to listen.

The meeting room was packed, as it had been all week. Turnout had been great, and the response so favorable. I enjoyed another great teaching, and when break time came I happened to spot a member of our staff who also enjoyed jet skiing.

Maybe I'll invite him along, I thought, and made my way across the room.

"Hey, Pastor John," he greeted me.

"Hey, Tom," I said. "I was going to go jet skiing during the afternoon session. Want to slip out and join me on our other jet ski?"

"That would be great!" he said, face brightening. He'd been working hard all week, as had many of our staff. Then a look of disappointment shadowed his countenance instead.

"Ah, I probably shouldn't," he said, sighing. "Too much to do heading into the weekend. I'd be distracted anyway, leaving the stuff I've got to do here."

"Okay. Your loss," I said jokingly, and wondering how many senior pastors encouraged their staff members to occasionally play hooky.

"I know, believe me," he said. "Have a good time. Jump some waves for me."

Normally, my jet ski companion was my second-oldest daughter, Tori. So many times I had called Tori on the way home from work and said simply, "Rack 'em up." She knew what it meant. In fact, she loved jet skiing so much that she offered to clean the skis and care for them back home. It was our special, shared hobby, and a great source of time together.

But at that very moment she was getting all four of her wisdom teeth out.

Probably too much to ask of her, I thought, picturing her riding the other jet ski with a swollen face. Not realistic.

The other conference attendees headed out to local restaurants for lunch, and I got in the car and went home. In the driveway, The Bulldog, our old Dodge truck, was already saddled up and ready to go, with the twin jet ski trailer attached and my XP Limited ratcheted down and ready to rock. Summer warmth had extended into September that year. In fact, it was September 11, and there had been some mentions of the anniversary of the terrorist attack on the news and in our sessions.

I tossed a couple of other supplies into the cab, then fired up The Bulldog and pulled away from the house. It was overcast, muggy and warm. *Bet the lake 'll be crowded,* I mused as I rumbled down the road. With each passing mile, I got more excited about what was ahead.

I picked up my phone to dial Wendy.

"Hello?"

"Hey, honey," I said. "I'm heading out to Lake Fenton. I want to try to get one more ride in this year."

"Okay," she said. "I remember you saying you wanted to do that. You're going by yourself?"

"Yes. How'd Tori's procedure go?" I asked.

"Fine," she said. "Her face is all swollen, of course. I'm going to get her something for the pain. She's hurting a lot. I think I'll have to run out to the pharmacy for some Motrin."

"Tell her I love her and I'll miss her today," I said. "I'll pick up a pizza on the way home and we can hang out and eat on the deck."

"Sounds good. Enjoy yourself," Wendy said.

"Thanks," I said, and really meant it. Wendy had been so supportive of my new hobby. The truth is, for better or worse, jet skiing was the first hobby I'd embraced since I was a kid. For two decades Wendy and I had poured our lives into planting and building a new church in Grand Blanc while at the same time raising our four kids. Those two huge tasks took so much focus that I felt I didn't have the time or energy for anything else. I didn't golf. I didn't fish. I didn't even collect anything.

"You need to get a hobby," Wendy often told me. She was a naturally creative person who always had some sewing project, artwork, gardening or reading to do. She was the kind who had tons of different things to do and not enough time to do them.

For me, my focus was always on ministry and family.

"Those are my hobbies," I objected when she tried to get me to spend time having fun.

"Yes, but you need to get your mind on something else

sometimes," Wendy counseled. "Let your brain take a break."

It was easy not to take her advice when we had no extra money. But as the kids grew older and our financial picture changed, the idea of indulging a long-held desire bubbled to the top of my mind.

Jet skis.

I had always wanted jet skis. In fact, I had always wanted to live in a cottage on a lake, and take advantage of all the recreation a lake had to offer — boating, fishing, swimming. But primarily jet skiing. Just thinking about riding one of those things across a lake at the highest speed possible made my spine thrill. It was a childhood dream that never let go.

When I mentioned the idea to Wendy, somewhat sheepishly, she surprised me with her support.

"For the longest time, your whole life has been about ministry and family, and that's it," she said. "I want you to have an outlet, a way to have fun. Now's the time. Go for it. Get yourself some toys."

So, I bought two machines, both used and in excellent condition. They were bumble-bee yellow and black. For my own pleasure, I got the XP Limited — a water-borne crotch rocket made for jetting and jumping. The other, a regular three-seat XP cruising machine, was less punchy and more predictable — even relaxed.

"Relaxed" was exactly what Wendy looked for in athletic experiences. As a teenager, she'd been as wild and crazy as any, jumping off a bridge into the river below, and that kind of thing. But over time she became more prone to motion sickness. A good day on a jet ski for her meant tooling slowly around the lake just beyond the docks, as if outlining the lake. Even on bikes and kayaks, which she liked, it was all about taking her time and avoiding quick, unexpected movements.

I was the opposite. Get me on a jet ski and I wanted the adrenaline rush, fast motion and cutting — all at once, if possible. It was how I was wired. Owning jet skis made me feel like a kid again. At night, I lay there thinking about ripping around the lake on them the next day. Just remembering that they were waiting for me after work put a smile on my face.

I was smiling as I drove The Bulldog toward Lake Fenton. The windows of the old truck were down, Christian music playing over the radio. My excitement was climbing. Random thoughts about life passed through my mind — some of the recent joys at our church, and a couple of issues I needed to take care of as a leader. I thought of our daughter Julia in Arizona training to enter the medical profession, and how much I missed having her around. I thought of Tori at home with her swollen face and four less teeth, and about Chloe enjoying life as a seven-year-old, and Micah, my only boy, growing into a young man trying to find his way.

The Bulldog seemed to pull herself into the gas station near the lake, knowing my routine. I hopped out to gas up the beast. I probably looked nothing like a traditional pastor in my shorts and water shoes. I felt like a boy heading out for an afternoon of fun.

Minutes later, back on the road, Lake Fenton came into view. Fenton is a long, windy, 845-acre lake lined with homes. As I approached the boat launch, I could see the lake was empty.

That's a surprise, I thought. *It's such a nice day, perfect for being on the water.*

On most days, particularly Fridays, Lake Fenton is buzzing with people. In the coves, boats anchor down and people jump off, swim around and have a good time. Now, for some reason, it was empty.

More room for me to unleash fury, I concluded, grinning.

Just glimpsing the water made my heart thump faster. Everything about water sports gets me going. Sometimes I would drive out of my way during the week just to lay eyes on it. When I got to the lake, all other thoughts disappeared. It was just me and the water.

At the boat launch I hopped out of the truck and began a well-worn process.

Untie the tie-downs that hold the ski onto the trailer. Make sure the plugs are in. (If you don't, the ski starts sinking.) Get back in the truck. Back the trailer slowly into the water.

With the trailer in the water, I jumped out of the truck, got on the XP, pushed it back from the trailer into the water, and turned it on. It bobbed and idled.

Love that sound!

When other people were around, Tori and I always got compliments on our machines. Tori detailed them regularly, so they were well maintained. We always dried them off and covered them before storing them between uses. As a result, they glistened in the sun.

Now I gently put the nose on the sand on the beach side of the dock so I could park the truck and trailer. Having done that I came back and stood next to the idling jet ski while strapping a life jacket to myself. Hanging from the jacket by a wire was a safety toggle that connected to the key and kept the ski running. If you fell off, the safety toggle would go with you and disable the engine so you could climb back on.

Ready to rock.

I slung a leg over the seat and pushed back into the water, anticipating the rush of that first turn of the throttle. Now the excitement wasn't ahead of me but all around me, just like the warm, humid air.

The moment had arrived.

***

Sports had always been my passion, whether it was baseball, football or mini-bikes. I loved motion, especially riding my bike on trails and up and down the streets of "Ghetto Greens," the semi-affectionate nickname for my childhood neighborhood, Village Greens, which sat behind a Lansing shopping mall.

Athletic stuff was just about all I cared about until the

day my sister, ten years older than me, came home looking different. For one thing, she was all wet, and it was February in Lansing, Michigan.

"What in the world? What are you doing?" I blurted out.

Her look of pure joy said it all.

"I'm saved!" she declared.

My sister had been living with us. Her young marriage was on the rocks. Now it appeared she'd gone crazy. I looked at her like, "What planet did you just arrive from?"

Still wet from her water baptism, she began sharing with me about Jesus, the Bible and eternal life. I had my game face on but I was freaking out on the inside. *I don't want to die and go to hell,* I kept thinking. Over the next few days, both my older brother and I decided to surrender our lives to Jesus Christ, and not just because we feared hell. My sister's new example and sincere words were persuasive.

Of course, I had no idea what being saved meant on a practical level, so my lifestyle after that decision looked pretty much like it had before. My parents were not church-going, and so the only time I talked with anyone about spiritual things was when my sister came home. Her marriage had been restored, and she and her husband were now living in Grand Rapids.

Our mom and dad divorced when I was ten. Then when I was a teen, Mom remarried a sheet metal model maker at Oldsmobile who made good money. We moved from the dumps to a great neighborhood. Instead of using third-generation spiked cleats in baseball, I now had a pair of new Nikes and a top-of-the-line A2000 baseball glove. I was excelling in baseball, to the point of realistically expecting a college scholarship. Even though my new stepdad was moody and sometimes violent when he drank, life became a little easier for my mom and me, especially financially.

Then there was my sister. "Go to that church near the house," she kept bugging me. *Yeah, whatever,* was my attitude. My heart was soft to God, but my life and schedule were pretty full at that point. Finally, to get her out of my ear, I went. The place was called Mount Hope Church. It was summertime. I was wearing my basketball shorts and a Michigan State jersey. I sat in the back row and watched older women lift their hands in worship, something I'd never seen.

Whoa. These people are serious, I thought.

As weird as it might have seemed, I could not deny the presence I felt in that place. I watched and listened to every little thing during the whole service. At the end, the pastor invited people forward to give their lives to Christ. I stood and walked to the front. Along the way it felt like a literal stack of bricks left my shoulders. The pastor laid hands on me and prayed for me. From that moment on, I was a different person.

Life-Preserving Principle #1

When you face a crisis, the local church has your back. Make sure you are part of a Bible-believing church.

I had become a Christian a few years before I started attending church — but it wasn't until I became part of a local church that I grew in my faith. Why? Because God created people to live in community. Ecclesiastes 4:9-10 says, "Two are better than one, because they have a good reward for their toil. For if they fall, one will lift up his fellow. But woe to him who is alone when he falls and has not another to lift him up!" (ESV)

How powerful is it to have a church full of friends who care about you and support you when you go through a crisis? Very powerful!

The apostle Paul tells us that Christians are part of a body. Even the smallest or seemingly most insignificant part is needed for the body to function.

For just as the body is one and has many members, and all the members of the body, though many, are one body, so it is with Christ. ... The eye cannot say to the hand, "I have no need of you," nor again the head to the feet, "I have no need of you." On the contrary, the parts of the body that seem to be weaker are indispensable, and on those parts of the body that we think less honorable we bestow the greater honor, and our unpresentable parts are treated with greater modesty, which our more presentable parts do not require. But God has so composed the body, giving greater honor to the part that lacked it, that there may be no division in the body, but that the members may have the same care for one another. If one member suffers, all suffer together; if one member is honored, all rejoice together.
1 Corinthians 12:12, 21-26 (ESV)

Also, the Bible tells us that God placed ministry gifts in the church so the members would be made stronger:

And he Himself gave some to be apostles, some prophets, some evangelists, and some pastors and teachers, for the equipping of the saints for the work of ministry, for the edifying of the body of Christ
Ephesians 4:11-12 (NKJV)

The leaders in a church are there to equip you for the work of the ministry. They will also equip you to face crisis when it comes. Many Christians are ill-equipped to face life challenges because they don't attend church regularly and are not part of a church family.

When my church family heard about my accident they were there for me, in prayer, and in support of my family.

Think of it in reverse as well: Not only do you need the church, but the church needs you! You will certainly have the privilege of helping someone else in their time of crisis. We all have gifts and experiences from which someone else can benefit.

I started taking Bible and leadership classes and going to prayer meetings with friends. I got involved in a campus ministry at Michigan State as a college-aged student and spent Friday and Saturday nights singing and sharing the gospel in dorms and the parking lots of the most popular bars. As much as I was passionate about sports, I had an equally intense passion to win souls and bring people to church.

At age nineteen I started a Bible study at work. I worked as the chauffeur of the Oldsmobile dealership, taking cars to customers in the capital in Lansing. At lunch, I was the leader of a Bible study attended by nearly twenty guys, most of them two and three times my age.

I'm amazed these guys take me seriously, I thought. *This is huge.*

Soon I started another Bible study with three mechanics. We met at a steak place once a week. I continued with the college campus ministry at Michigan State.

It became obvious that I should get more ministry training, so after a year attending Grand Valley State University on a baseball scholarship, I went down to Rhema Bible Training Center in Tulsa, Oklahoma. I had never been around so many people who were so on fire for the Lord.

This is exactly the kind of person I want to be, I thought. *This is awesome.*

There, I met a girl who happened to be from Michigan: Wendy. She was from a family of eleven kids and had flown down to Tulsa in a small four-seat airplane piloted by a generous older couple who was paying her way to attend. God was at work in her family. A number of her siblings had met Christ and were attending a good church in nearby Wisconsin. Wendy was as radical for the Lord as I was. It didn't take us long to see that we belonged together.

After completing our schooling, we headed back to Michigan, were married and began serving at Mount Hope Church, the same church where I had walked the aisle. It was being led now by a young pastor named Dave Williams. At his request, I taught some evening services and led a small group. Then one day, Dave surprised me.

"John, I have a vision to plant churches like Mount Hope Church throughout Michigan and the world, and I think you'd make a great church planter," he said. "You'd be the first one, our guinea pig. What do you think?"

"Let's do it," I said.

Wendy and I were primed and ready. This was the right open door. We moved to Grand Blanc, an hour away from Lansing, and started the hard, real work of pioneering a church. My first office was in the storage room of an office building and could only be accessed through the bathroom. Those were our great beginnings.

It didn't take long to start growing. We immediately began raising up leaders for various ministries: youth, children's, worship and so on. From day one we were about empowering people and releasing them into ministry. It was a leadership-driven church, and we gave to support world missions and missionaries.

Our young church continued to grow. We met in an old rented parks and rec building (which has since been turned into a parking lot) and attendance steadily doubled year after year. We trained everyone we could as a leader, then watched with joy as they made a difference in the lives of others.

There were tough times, too. Sometimes staff members transitioned out, and occasionally a transition was rough. Our area of Michigan, Grand Blanc (which is near Flint) was one that was first hit and the last to recover when the economy bottomed out. This was due to the area's dependence on the automobile industry. We had seen a number of people leave due to job changes, and our budget sometimes shrank drastically as people's wages were cut in half, or worse.

But we always made it through; God had seen to that. Now, twenty-one years later, we had a beautiful facility visible from the highway, and forty-eight acres of land to use. Better than that, we had hundreds of committed people, a great reputation and positive influence in the community. God was clearly at work.

***

Although I loved being a pastor and building a church,

when I turned my XP Limited toward the lake and tugged on the throttle, every other thought faded into the background.

Think I'll whip around for a couple of hours, jump off and swim in shallow areas for a bit, then maybe catch some wakes off other boats, if there are any, I thought. *Then, back to the house for pizza with the family — except for Tori who probably can't chew real food yet.*

Astride the powerful 951 cc engine, I nosed into deeper waters and took the speed higher.

I'm so glad I had that steel impeller installed, I thought. *An insane amount of torque is just what I'm looking for right now. Let's unleash fury.*

I pulled the handle back further and, like a wild beast startled from its lair, the machine and I burst forward.

I cut a straight line across the lake, heading roughly north, and playing a bit with the dynamics, leaning from side to side and feeling the Limited respond to each small move. Wide open water surrounded me on each side. The wind had picked up considerably and was gusting across the lake. But it didn't make much difference in my riding. The ski seemed to glide out of the water as we skimmed over the surface. Houses passed by on either side like hunkered-down spectators.

*I really hope we can get a cottage on a lake like this up
north someday,* I thought, dreaming my childhood dream.
*I can picture having a boat, a dock, the jet skis, and fish-
ing rods in the garage.*

For fun, I slowed down slightly, then turned sharply left,
leaning in so I didn't flip over. Then I whipped around the
other way, carefully managing the throttle as I did. I did
a full circle, feeling the g's pulling at me as I gripped the
handlebars.

Man, I love this!

After the turns I caught sight of open lake ahead of me
and hammered the throttle again, bursting into the space.
Nothing else in my life gave me such a feeling of motion,
power, and freedom.

Just then I bumped over a couple of ripples. I was close to
the north end now, and ahead of me was a boat — not just
any boat, but a 24-foot Scarab twin engine power boat,
like nothing I had ever seen on Lake Fenton. This boat —
beautiful white, with white interior — was made for open
oceans, not landlocked little lakes in the Midwest. The
pilot was leaving some wake behind him, so I jetted and
jumped them a few times. Most of the time, boaters didn't

mind you hitting their wakes. Courtesy, and the law, state that you should stay a couple of hundred feet away from boats. I had been yelled at a couple of times, especially by lady pilots when I got too close.

"You should know better! You're a grown man," one woman scolded me. "You could really get hurt on that thing."

But as I looked ahead I saw something unusual. The pilot of the huge boat was standing up and waving me over.

Wonder what that's about? I thought and gunned toward him. I was already starting to dream of those first couple slices of pizza, and maybe a stop to get a Coke on the rocks at that gas station.

I was now close enough to hear the slightly-built, young pilot who had beckoned me over.

"I'll create waves for you and you can have some fun," he shouted.

That was a rare offer. Most boaters ignored jet skiers. I glanced at his engines. Those two powerhouses were well-armed to dig nice, big, watery trenches for me to explode over in my jumps.
"Sweet," I said. "Thanks!"

I turned around to put a little distance between us. He turned to his steering wheel and hit the gas. Sure enough, those engines were more than up for the task, plowing a deep, beautiful wake in front of me.

Now we're talking, I thought, and took aim.

Back and forth I went, jumping three feet in the air, then four feet. The wind was still heavy but it only added to the feeling as I hung there in mid-air.

This is way better than I was expecting, I thought, and continued to launch over the wake, back and forth.

After a few minutes, the pilot turned back and headed to the boat launch.

"Thanks!" I yelled back. He throttled up and sped away quickly, leaving a huge rolling wake in front of me as one last favor.

This is going to be epic, I thought. The wakes he was creating were unlike any I had ever seen. The jet ski actually went down into them before rocketing up and piercing the air. And the final one — it was the biggest of all. I took aim at the big roller and felt pure thrill course through my body as the nose of the ski took me down into the trough and then up the side wall into the sky.

On his boat, Brian, the owner and pilot, was already well north of me but happened to glance back as I launched. He was heading to the gas station to fill the boat, then going to town for a haircut and meeting his wife for dinner. His mind was already on other things when, for some reason, he looked over his shoulder. What he saw greatly concerned him.

I had taken the wake at full speed, hit it and flown upward. That was the last thing I remember. The jet ski snapped back at me on impacting the wake's wall, and because I didn't know the right technique for hitting a wake that big — with one foot placed on the front of the ski and the other at the back — it slammed me in the face.

I came flying out of that scoop already unconscious, the jet ski engine still thrusting water behind it and propelling it, and me, upward.

The back of that thing must be eight feet out of the air! Brian thought. *That means the rider is at least fifteen feet over the water.*

He watched as I flew off the jet ski, landed face down on it, then fell over the front as the jet ski landed on top of me.

That doesn't look good, Brian thought. Any idea of gassing up and getting a quick haircut disappeared. He watched as the jet ski capsized and my body floated next to it, unresponsive. Immediately, he stopped the boat and turned it around.

It took him several minutes to reach me because he was so far ahead by now, and strong winds had already pushed my body into a shallow area, four feet deep, near Log Cabin Point. Brian's boat engines were so powerful that they couldn't operate in shallow water — they would pull up sand and debris and damage the boat props. He came as close as he could, stopping a hundred feet away or so, and saw my limp body floating face down, as if I were eating seaweed. Only my feet were sticking out of the water. My life jacket was not even remotely doing its job.

Man, this is bad, Brian thought as he shut off the boat and jumped into the water fully clothed. He swam over swiftly, took hold of my body and turned me right-side up. It was a gruesome sight.

His face looks like pizza, he thought. *He's not breathing.*

Blood was coming out of my ears and eyes. My lower lip was hanging down on my chin. He felt my neck for a pulse. Nothing.

He's already dead, he thought dispassionately. *Might as well drag him back to my boat because I need a phone.*

This wasn't the first time Brian had dealt with an emergency of this magnitude. For whatever reason, he'd come upon scenes like this half a dozen times, and in all but one of them he had successfully performed life-saving measures, though he lacked any real training. There had been heart attack victims, stroke victims, a near-drowning on that very lake in a cove, and a motorcycle accident in another state. All Brian had in the way of medical knowledge was CPR training back in the sixth grade. But somehow, he'd been able to pull people back from death.

Now, as he took hold of my life jacket and began to drag me to his boat, he felt a calm come over him. Even more than the other times, he felt like he was on autopilot. Like someone else was driving the boat. Like God, whom he didn't know, was guiding his every move.

But the wind worked against him as he tried to swim and drag me, still face down in the water, toward his boat. The boat was now two hundred feet away, having drifted with the steady winds, and Brian was fully clothed and a slim five feet, eight inches tall and 146 pounds. I had at least sixty pounds on him on a normal day. Having taken in large amounts of water, I was much heavier than that, and dead weight.

There's no one else on the lake, Brian observed, looking around for help. *At least I looked back and saw this guy's accident. Nineteen years on this lake and I don't remember rubber-necking like that just to watch a jet skier before.*

It was taking longer than he wanted, and costing him more energy, but he continued to swim and drag me simultaneously. Finally, he reached his boat. Brian didn't know what to do next. He treaded water, held my body near with one hand and considered his options. I was far too heavy for him to pull into the boat alone. While considering what to do, he turned me upright in the water and saw some sign of life in my face.

Wait, maybe this guy's not dead after all, he thought.

Instinctively, he put his mouth on my bloody face and tried to push air into my lungs. Because we were floating and I was unconscious, it didn't work. He quickly thought about how he might perform chest compressions in the water, but that, too, would be impossible.

Then he caught sight of the metal bar that connected his two powerful engines and enabled them to turn in unison.

That's it, he thought. Without wasting time he stuffed my body between the engines, found a strap on my life jacket and tried to hook it over the bar.

I've just got to get his face to stay out of the water, he thought as he attempted to hook the straps together. The wind kept working against him, as did the difficulty of hoisting a body out of the water while keeping himself afloat. Somehow, he got the straps to click together and hold. My body was now suspended between the engines with my face out of water, still unconscious and not breathing.

Without delaying, Brian somehow knew to open the padding on my life jacket so he could access my chest. Then, taking a deep breath, he began pounding me as hard as he could with his fist, right in the heart. A strange certainty told him he was doing the right thing — that his goal was to punch me in the chest as many times as he could to kick start my heart and get it pumping blood.

Come on, man. Live!

Brian punched as the boat kept drifting, making it hard to keep his balance. He grabbed it with one hand, kicked his legs underwater to stay afloat, and simultaneously pounded my chest, hoping the life jacket straps would continue to hold my body up.

I'm not sure this is doing any good, he thought. He

stopped to feel for a pulse. Nothing. Back to work. In the back of his mind he counted his hits.

Twenty ... thirty... forty ...

My body jerked with each landed punch, but nothing happened.

Fifty ... sixty... seventy ...

Brian was tiring out, but kept swinging. My heart was at the water line so each punch splashed water everywhere, creating even more confusion. Still I hung limp.

If I can just get the water out of his lungs, maybe he'll have a chance, he thought.

Eighty ... ninety ... one hundred ...

Three minutes of straight punching had elapsed, and Brian felt like a boxer at the end of a difficult first round. But he was driven by adrenaline now, and something stronger: hope.

Just keep going, man, he told himself. *One hundred ten ... one hundred twenty ...*

Why am I doing this? This guy is gone, he questioned.

Still, he kept hitting me as hard as he could. His knuckles and fingers ached with injury. At times, he used his elbow instead of his hand to keep the drumbeat going against my chest. He could barely find the strength to keep himself afloat anymore, but his focus was on that small area, the few square inches of flesh above my heart.

One hundred thirty ... one hundred forty ... Come on, man! I thought I saw life in you. Wake up! One hundred fifty ...

Suddenly, something whacked Brian on the head. I had come alive and unwittingly thrown a roundhouse punch at him. Now I was clawing and punching Brian's face. I was unconscious and must have been in panic mode.

Whoa! Whoa, whoa! he said and tried to back out of my range. I eyed him wildly, as if he were an enemy, and kept pummeling and clutching at him.

Wouldn't that be ironic, if this guy drowns me after I try to save him? he thought.

At the same time, I began throwing up voluminous amounts of lake water and blood. Brian pulled away and watched astounded as this continued for more than a minute. After the vomiting and punching subsided he allowed himself to feel a small flicker of success, but when he re-approached me I hammered his face and gouged his eyes again.

Ow! Dude! Okay, okay! he thought. *This isn't a fair fight. You're hanging from your straps, you're bigger than me, and I'm fully clothed, treading water and trying to help you. Please, don't kill me.*

Exhausted, he pulled away from me again and hoisted himself onto the swim platform of his boat. Just then, a small Baja boat cruised by some distance away. The other pilot looked over.

"Hey, call 911," Brian yelled. "I've got a guy who got in an accident."

The other man held up his phone to confirm he was calling.

Now that I know there are professionals coming, where should I take him? Brian calculated. *I can't fire up the engines with him back there. I really should try to get him to shore.*

Instantly, an idea came to mind. He shed clothes and jumped back into the water in his boxers. As soon as he came to me, I began swinging again, not conscious of what I was doing. Between my swings, Brian reached onto my life jacket and pulled off the safety toggle to the jet ski.

Got it.

Verifying that I was safely hanging from the metal bar, he swam over to the jet ski which had drifted in the wind a couple hundred feet away. But it was upside down, which for a jet ski is bad news. When a jet ski gets flipped over, it's difficult to start again. (To have any good chance, you must flip it back over the correct way. Even then you could only hope for the best.)

Brian reached my XP Limited, somehow knew which way to turn it right-side up, put in the safety toggle and started it right up. If I had been conscious to see it, I probably wouldn't have believed how easy he made it look. He motored back over to the boat, got off the jet ski and into the water next to me.

"I'm going to unhook you now," he said, not knowing if I could hear him. "I want to try to pull you into shore."

This time, I mumbled something back. Brian understood it as, "What happened to me?"

"You hurt yourself on your jet ski," Brian said. "I'm here and trying to rescue you and help you."

"Thank you," I said.

"That's nice to hear," he replied.

I had a vague sense that something was hanging down my chin, so I kept putting my lip back up in its right place. It continued to fall down on my chin. Then I went into coughing and vomiting spasms, gaining and losing consciousness in a haze.

"I'm going to put my foot through your life jacket and gently bring you to shore," Brian said. "Fire and rescue is going to be there. An ambulance is coming."

Brian unhooked my straps and I slumped back into the lake. Brian swiftly grabbed a couple of floating noodles from his boat and put them under my arms to try to keep me up. Then he jumped up on the Limited, reached around to pull me closer, then carefully hooked his right ankle inside my life jacket. Confident enough to continue, he let the jet ski idle forward as he kept hold of me with his foot. Slowly, he towed me to shore, six hundred feet away.

As we drew nearer, I came to consciousness and heard sirens and commotion.

It's not that bad, I remember thinking. *Maybe I just hurt myself on a jet ski. I don't know why they called in all of Genesee County EMS.*

After some time, my body scraped the bank. Brian hopped off and pulled me the rest of the way to shore. Paramedics were walking swiftly but quietly down the yard of one of the lake houses, and police officers and fire fighters were behind them. Brian, stunned and completely spent, sat down next to me.

"Man, I'm so tired. This has taken everything out of me. I'm going to need a cigarette," he said, groaning.

"Go for it," I mumbled.

The paramedics put a neck brace on me and talked soothingly as they did everything.
"Now we're going to put this board underneath you. Now we're going to carry you up to the ambulance."

Inside the vehicle, all the lake noise disappeared. I lay there with little idea of what had happened, and why I was in an ambulance.

"We have you now. You're in good hands," a paramedic said. "Everything's going to be all right."

I heard them report my condition to the hospital as we

rumbled down the road. Consciousness came and went, until at the hospital I saw a huge light over me, and seven or eight doctors around my bed.

"Yeah, we're going to need a plastic surgeon. Now," the man who seemed to be in charge said. Then I was out. Back at Lake Fenton, Brian realized he was on shore with my jet ski while his boat was floating freely in the lake. He had expended so much energy that he was seeing colors and hallucinating. After collapsing on the bank, he had no memory of the paramedics putting me on a stretcher or taking me away.

My boat's still floating way out on the lake, was all he could summon. Then deeper, the thought came as a question: *Why does God always put me in these situations? Is this a spiritual thing? Maybe someday I'll figure it out.*

CHAPTER 2

Wendy was driving to Rite-Aid to buy Motrin for Tori's aching face when the call came from Eric Austermann, a board member at the church. By the sound of it, he seemed to be at a high school football game, which made sense because it was a Friday in September.

"Wendy, I just got a call on the care phone," he said above the crowd din. "It's about John."

The care phone was the 24-hour line at the church which rang to a cell phone that was always carried by a pastoral staff member. It handled incoming emergency calls or needs that just couldn't wait.

"John was in a jet ski accident and they took him to Genesys," Eric continued as the crowd cheered for a play behind him. "He's at the hospital right now. They had to pull him from the water. They're looking for you. You need to get over there."

Wendy could hear people talking happily about the game in the background, in stark contrast to the disconcerting message Eric was relating.

"Okay. Thanks," she said. "I'll head right over."

No wonder John was so late, she thought. For the past hour, she and the girls had been waiting for him to walk in with pizzas, or at least call and give an estimated time of arrival. She turned the car around and headed for the hospital. On the way there, Eric's wife called back.

"Wendy, don't worry about the kids," she said. "I'll go over to the house and make sure Tori gets what she needs. I'll feed the girls dinner and put them to bed."

"Thank you," Wendy said, deeply gratified at the thoughtfulness and help. As she drove on toward the hospital she had little information to go on — *they pulled him from the lake* — but her mind was besieged with questions. *How bad is it? What if this is the end? What am I going to do without him?* Racing ahead to every scenario, her mind tried to create a picture of a future without John, to somehow make the situation okay.

Wait a minute, Wendy thought, arresting her spinning thoughts. *I can't think like this. This is one of those times where you either believe what you believe, or you don't. I have to believe God's word. If there's ever a time to cling to his promises, it's now!*

Life-Preserving Principle #2

When in a crisis, "think on these things."

When disaster strikes, our minds can run wild. Most of the time, our thoughts run to the worst possible scenarios. As a believer, this is where we have to make a choice to decide what we will dwell upon. Yes, it's a choice. Your mind is like a movie screen. And you get to choose what word pictures will play there. The Bible is clear about this choice:

… since the weapons of our warfare are not worldly, but are powerful through God for the demolition of strongholds. We demolish arguments and every high-minded thing that is raised up against the knowledge of God, taking every thought captive to obey Christ.
2 Corinthians 10:4-5 (HCSB)

Notice how active that is — we have to take every thought captive to obey Christ. Any thought that rises up against the knowledge of God has to be captured. Especially in a crisis, we can't let our thoughts run to worst-case scenarios.

What should we think about? The Bible makes it clear:

Don't worry about anything; instead, pray about everything. Tell God what you need, and thank him for all he has done. Then you will experience God's peace, which exceeds anything we can understand. His peace will guard your hearts and minds as you live in Christ Jesus. And now, dear brothers and sisters, one final thing. Fix your thoughts on what is true, and honorable, and right, and pure, and lovely, and admirable. Think about things that are excellent and worthy of praise. Keep putting into practice all you learned and received from me—everything you heard from me and saw me doing. Then the God of peace will be with you.
Philippians 4:6-9 (NLT)

In other words, don't worry. Pray — and pray about everything. Tell God what you need. The moment Wendy received the call about my accident she had a choice worry or pray. She could have worried about the future or she could "tell God what she needed," also known as prayer. Right then, Wendy needed me to be okay. She needed me to breathe, to not have brain damage and for the water to leave my lungs. She needed me to live and not die. So instead of letting fear and worry take over she prayed.

Then what? Fix your thoughts on what is true, honorable, right, pure, lovely and admirable. Think on things that are excellent and worthy of praise. What would an "excellent" result look like in our circumstance? Me rising from that deathbed totally healed. So that's what she thought about.

Wendy exhaled deeply, steered the car into the parking lot and inwardly stood her ground against a bombardment of unwanted thoughts. Mental strength had been built into Wendy's life at an early age. She was the eighth of eleven children in a tiny house with a father who drank too much, and a mom who suffered three nervous breakdowns. In a very real way, Wendy and her siblings had survived their childhoods.

Wendy came from a line of Belgian and Swedish farmers who eked out an existence in the UP — the Upper Peninsula of Michigan. Their manner was reserved to the point of being stoic and unemotional. Except for the anger. The defining fact of her home was their father's angry drunkenness. It poisoned the atmosphere with fear, and perhaps contributed to his wife's mental illness. Though Wendy's mother kept the 1,100-square-foot home immaculate, their father would come home and find a stack of dishes in the sink, and he would rouse the household with yelling at 2 a.m. and demand it be fixed.

Adding to the stress was the birth of a son who was mentally disabled when their mother was in her mid-forties.

He was given up for adoption, but the stress remained. Their mother sometimes went to the hospital for weeks because of mental issues. During these times, the kids cooked and cared for themselves. When she returned, Wendy would come home from high school to find her weeping on her bed.

As a teenager, Wendy spent a summer away, lifeguarding in a nearby town. She returned to find that some of her friends had attended a tent revival meeting and dedicated their lives to Jesus. They started inviting Wendy and her siblings to a youth group at a church across a bridge in Wisconsin. The church was started by a graduate of Rhema Bible Training Center in Tulsa. Wendy noticed a real difference in her friends and started attending the church, then participating on the worship team. Within a few months, her whole outlook on life had changed. The positive, powerful preaching of men like Kenneth Hagin, whose cassette tapes she listened to endlessly, was the perfect antidote for the relentless negativity of most everything else around her. Knowing that God had given His Word and His promises made life so much better. Suddenly she had tools to deal with bad situations. Things stopped feeling out of control. She could lean on the Lord and trust Him. No matter what happened at home, there was always hope.

The church became their surrogate family, and the teaching that flowed there set a new foundation for sixteen-year-old Wendy. Within five years, almost everyone in her family gave their lives to Jesus and experienced profound, positive change as a result.

Life-Preserving Principle #3

When in a crisis, be a doer of the word.

Earlier, I referenced Philippians 4:9. After we get our thoughts on the right things, Paul then tells us to "keep putting into practice all you learned and received from me."

The apostle James tells us the same thing:

But don't just listen to God's word. You must do what it says. Otherwise, you are only fooling yourselves. For if you listen to the word and don't obey, it is like glancing at your face in a mirror. You see yourself, walk away, and forget what you look like. But if you look carefully into the perfect law that sets you free, and if you do what it says and don't forget what you heard, then God will bless you for doing it.
James 1:22-25 (NLT)

I like to tell my congregation that as much as you comb

your hair, you need to renew your mind to the Word of God. But we can't just hear it. It's not until you put it into practice, engage it actively, that the Word of God transforms your life and changes your circumstances.

Again, it's not enough to hear God's word and think you know it. We have to do it. Especially in the crises of life, it is the doers of the word who overcome. These are the moments when our tests become testimonies.

The first big change and challenge for Wendy after becoming a Christian, was walking in love and forgiveness toward her father. The first time God ever spoke to her in an unmistakable way, was to say, "You have to go home and tell your dad you love him." She was seventeen and did not want to do that. For years, she had watched her dad pour his money into alcohol while the rest of the family went without necessary things. They didn't even have their own washer and dryer, but had to go to the laundromat and take up an entire wall of machines to do laundry. He would also yell at them for being bad kids, even when they were well-behaved and good students. Wendy and her sister were both salutatorians in their graduating high school classes.

But as Wendy pondered what she had heard from God, she decided she really believed that His love made you bigger than yourself. She obeyed, and the simple act

of telling her dad she loved him broke chains of anger
and bitterness in her own heart. She felt a new perspective — that her father was just a person dealing with his
own problems. He had served in the Korean War as the
driver who brought lieutenants to the battlefield, and as
a mechanic who fixed Jeeps. She had little idea what he
had experienced that might have shaped him. And she
received good things from him, too, like her love of music and a giftedness in that area. He had a beautiful tenor
voice and played trumpet in a polka band. She discovered
the strength to love him the way God loved him and put
the bad experiences of their home aside.

Wendy also had to learn to bless the girls in her high
school class who were notoriously mean. So she went
home and hung Scriptures all over her wall as reminders:
"Don't return evil for evil but overcome evil with good."
"Be kind one to another." As a very young Christian she
saw that you could either put God's word into practice
or keep looking at the circumstances. One or the other
would define you — it was your choice.

Later, after years of praying for her father to come to
Jesus and stop drinking, a strange thing happened. He
developed dementia and simply forgot to drink. After he
died, Wendy was in a meeting in Detroit, and the speaker,
who had a prophetic gift, said something out of the blue
that struck Wendy's heart: "There's somebody here won-

dering if your dad who passed away is in heaven, and the Lord told me to tell you that he is." Wendy was certain the word was for her.

Her life was so powerfully impacted by the church in Wisconsin that when Wendy graduated high school she decided to attend Rhema Bible Training Center in Tulsa — but she had no money. The miracle arrived via a couple in the church, dairy farmers who also worked at the local newspaper. They asked if they could pay her tuition. It was a significant amount of money, but they believed God would provide. Not only that but they flew her down to Oklahoma in their crop-duster-like four-seater plane, stopping only to gas up and wait out a storm in Nebraska.

In Tulsa, Wendy found herself surrounded by people with the same goals and passion for believing God's Word and living by faith. In classes and at church she heard messages every week from leaders in that movement.

And she met me, an Italian guy from lower Michigan, which was a world away from the UP, culturally speaking. I asked her to marry me on Valentine's Day, six months after we started dating. She agreed, and it was the best fit. My mother became like a mother to Wendy. We headed back to Lansing together to start our life journey.

***

Now, as Wendy arrived at Genesys Regional Medical
Center, the lessons of all those difficult times came back
to help. Yes, her husband had been in a jet ski accident.
Yes, the circumstances were real. But God's Word is
always bigger than circumstances.

*I know I'm not in control of what's happening in there,
but God is at work in this situation,* she thought as she
crossed the parking lot toward the entrance. *As for me, I
will put the worst possibilities aside and believe for the
best. I believe that John will live and not die. I believe he
is healed completely.*

She took the elevator to the fourth floor Intensive Care
Unit and glimpsed me on a stretcher, with a tube down
my throat, unconscious and being rolled into another
room. The preview steeled her nerves as an ER doctor, a
woman, greeted her and invited her into a little conference room.

"Wendy, here's what we know," she said. "John was
found headfirst in the water. He'd been that way for a
number of minutes. He took in a lot of water. When he
came in to the hospital he was breathing and even trying
to talk, but then he started coughing and has coughed up
a significant amount of water. We had to intubate him.
We needed to do something fast because he was having

a hard time breathing. I could tell his lungs were filling with water. We don't know if there's brain damage because he's not conscious anymore. You're welcome to wait here in the waiting room until I find out if it's okay to see him."

"Okay," Wendy said, taking in the details as best she could. In her mind, she kept returning to what she chose to believe — that I would recover fully. The ER doctor dismissed herself, and Wendy stepped into the waiting room. Two staff members, Eric Anderson and Joe Mead, were already there. They had left dinner to rush to the hospital.

"Wendy, you okay?" they said.

"Yeah, I'll be fine," she said.

"We're calling people and getting them praying," Eric said, his phone lighting up with responses.

"Others are coming down here," Joe added.

The ER doctor came in and nodded at them.

"You can see John for a few moments, if you wish," she said.

"Can they come with me?" Wendy asked, motioning to Eric and Joe.

"Sure," said the doctor with just a slight hesitation. When Eric had arrived at the hospital moments earlier, the front desk attendant had been smiling and cheerful until he said he was there to see John Galinetti. Then her countenance fell discernibly. *She knows something,* he thought.

"I need to go talk to a doctor and see if he can have visitors," she said, suddenly more even in her response.

While he waited, Eric called his wife on the phone.

"This is more serious than we thought," he said. "The nurse looked at me like she thought he was a goner. We need everybody praying."

Now he, Wendy and Joe proceeded to a nearby room in the ICU. There I lay with my upper body raised, unconscious and with a large breathing apparatus obscuring much of my face.

Man, he looks bad, Eric thought, and glanced at Wendy to see how she was absorbing the sight. Wendy looked at me for a moment as if continuing an internal conversation, then lay a hand on my lower leg affectionately.

"Let's pray for him," Eric offered. He put his hand on me as well and prayed a prayer straight from Ephesians.

"John, the Spirit that raised Christ from the dead lives in you," he declared. "Resurrection life is in you. You will live and not die."

His words were spoken softly but intensely. I don't remember hearing them, but I know they penetrated my spirit.

"Amen," said Wendy.

"Amen," said Joe.

They walked back to the waiting room, and half a dozen people from the church were there, with more arriving by the minute.

"Looks like we might take the place over," said Elaine, my secretary, with a slight grin. Wendy noticed that many people were tapping on their phones.

"Everyone's texting our contacts and starting prayer chains," she said. "There's probably fifty people praying already."

The atmosphere in the room was not anxious or hushed but positive, upbeat, even confident. It didn't feel like an intensive care unit; it felt like the family of God.

Thank you, Lord, for this support, Wendy thought. *These people are helping me so much just by being here and believing with me. I couldn't do it without them.*

"Let's have everyone circle up for a moment," said Wendy to people nearby, and they spread the word. Normally, I was the leader out front giving people direction. Now Wendy knew it was her job. People formed a circle around the waiting room, which was quickly growing too small for everyone who was arriving.

"I know it looks bad," Wendy started, "but today, I choose to believe God's promises over my husband's life, and John is going to live."

"Amen," said several.

Others spoke their agreement: "Yes, Lord." "We receive it."

"I know a bunch of people are praying already, and I wanted us to take some time as a group and lift John up to the Lord," she said. "So, I'll just begin. Lord, we thank you for this day. We rejoice even in this circumstance, and we ask you to intervene and restore John's health to what it was before the accident. Be with him in his bed. Help his lungs to recover, his heart, his mind — everything. Thank you, in Jesus' name."

Someone else immediately began praying earnestly out loud, then another and another. They clasped hands and formed a circle of faith that must have been a powerful thing to behold. One by one, people spoke forth prayers to God, standing on the authority of his word, quoting favorite verses and promises, claiming the healing they believed would come. Then they thanked God for my full recovery. After a moment of quiet, Wendy spoke again.

"God, I choose to believe your promises today."

The silence was almost reverent. Then she began to sing a song that had been on her mind all week, and which seemed to connect with her heart in a special way.

"Your name is a strong and mighty tower," she sang as the rest joined in. It was a beautiful melody, and in that moment, Wendy knew that God had given her the song to hold onto. When no word was forthcoming from the doctors, when I was unconscious and my status uncertain, Wendy had a song in the night.

Life-Preserving Principle #4

When in crisis, sing.

At your darkest times, God will give you a song, if you'll
listen. We see this principle throughout God's word. In
the Old Testament, the psalmist wrote beautifully,

I waited patiently for the Lord to help me,
    and he turned to me and heard my cry.
He lifted me out of the pit of despair,
    out of the mud and the mire.
He set my feet on solid ground
    and steadied me as I walked along.
He has given me a new song to sing,
    a hymn of praise to our God.
Many will see what he has done and be amazed.
    They will put their trust in the Lord.
(Psalm 40:1-3, NLT)

That's what God does — gives us a new song to sing.
Sometimes it's a song in the night, like the one Paul
and Silas sang in jail at midnight in the cruel prison in
Philippi. They had been beaten, accused and wrongly put
in shackles. Yet still, God gave them a song in the night
which became the anthem of their deliverance.

That was just God doing what he promised:
By day the Lord directs his love,
     at night his song is with me—
     a prayer to the God of my life.
(Psalm 42:8, NIV)

"At night his song is with me …" Music is powerful.
God created it to be that way. It has the power to lift your
spirit, inspire change, and express your faith. For Wendy,
that's what happened the night of my accident.

"Nothing has the power to save but your name."

Spontaneously, the group applauded, underlining their
belief in the words. Then they hugged each other and
fell into conversation. Many chose to stay until midnight
before heading home to catch some sleep.

Two thousand miles away, in Palm Desert, California,
one of the couples to receive a call for prayer was Harry
and Cheryl Salem, longtime friends of ours. The Salem's
are a powerful ministry family and know what it means
to hear from God and walk it out. They were heading into
a furniture store that September evening when the phone
rang.

"Hello?"

"Harry, this is Ted from Mount Hope Church Grand Blanc."

Ted Milian was a key staff member at the church.

"Hi, Ted. How are you?" Harry asked.

"I'm doing well, but John has been in an accident. A jet ski accident. He hit a wake and landed bad. He was underwater for a while," said Ted.

"John Galinetti has been in an accident," Harry spoke off the phone to Cheryl.

Cheryl immediately started praying and asking the Lord to reveal his will in the situation.

"What's his condition?" Harry asked Ted.

"The doctors say it's not good. He might have as little as two percent chance to live," Ted said.

"Ted, hold the line," Harry said, then to Cheryl: "We need to pray right now."

Life-Preserving Principle #5

Remember that there is no distance in prayer.

Think about how powerful is prayer, that no matter where you are on the planet, you can pray to God in the name of Jesus — and receive answers! People all over the world prayed for me. People in Ireland, people in Africa, people in Palm Springs, California, and people in Fort Lauderdale, Florida. Everywhere God's people prayed, God heard their prayers and answered.

You may be far away physically from the person or situation you are burdened to pray about; but God is not distant. He is right there with you — and with them.

You may think, "I'm just one person, what can I do?" Pray!

Are any of you suffering hardships? You should pray. Are any of you happy? You should sing praises. Are any of you sick? You should call for the elders of the church to come and pray over you, anointing you with oil in the name of the Lord. Such a prayer offered in faith will heal the sick, and the Lord will make you well. And if you have committed any sins, you will be forgiven.
Confess your sins to each other and pray for each other so that you may be healed. The earnest prayer of a righteous person has great power and produces wonderful results. Elijah was as human as we are, and yet when he prayed earnestly that no rain would fall, none fell for three and a half years! Then, when he prayed again, the

sky sent down rain and the earth began to yield its crops.
James 5:13-18 (NLT)

Praying is a very important way we behave as doers of
the word. James asks, "Are any of you suffering hardships? If the answer is yes, then pray!" Why? Because the
"earnest prayer of a righteous person has great power and
produces wonderful results!"

Sometimes it's tempting to think that you are just one
human on the planet, and what possible difference could
you make? The answer is, a whole lot. Elijah was as human as we are, and yet he prayed earnestly and got amazing results.

In a crisis, pray earnestly. It's powerful. God hears and
answers.

It didn't matter that the Salems were out shopping for
furniture for their son and daughter-in-law, who were
recently engaged. God's business came first. They ducked
inside and told the store employee who approached that
they were on an emergency call. Ted stayed on the line
while they sought God together.

It didn't take long for Cheryl to nod affirmatively.

"Ted, this is not unto death," she said. "I keep hearing the

Holy Spirit say it's not unto death. Do not look at this as John is dead but that he is alive and God can do a miracle with him."

"Yes," Harry agreed. "Ted, you said someone saw him in the weeds and dragged him to shore."

"Right," said Ted.

"That's the first miracle," Harry said. "That's how you know you're in the midst of an even greater miracle. Remember in the building of temple under Zerubbabel in the Bible. They actually stopped and began to worship in the middle of it, because God was doing a miracle. So, begin to thank God for the miracle he is doing right now in John's life."

Cheryl jumped in. "I feel that by morning you're going to see a definite turn in his condition," she said. "I'm not saying that just to encourage everybody. I'm saying that because I believe it's assurance from the throne room of God that John will live. I feel that as clear as I'm talking to you."

"Thank you," said Ted. "Thank you."

After a few more minutes praying together, Ted hung up with assurances that he would keep them posted when he knew anything more. For the next hour and a half, the Salems sat on a sectional sofa in the store, not to choose furniture but to intercede for me non-stop. They emailed their prayer chains to do the same.

"John will live and not die," they declared over and over.

Wendy and I had become friends with the Salems in the mid-1990s. Harry was from Flint, and Cheryl had gained national recognition when she won the Miss America pageant, representing Mississippi. Our children were the same age, and the Salems often came to our church to minister and spend time with us.

"John will live and not die," they said with complete confidence that the words were true — though their only evidence was the word of the Lord.

Back in Michigan, Deb Tangen sat in her office at an emergency medical services company in downtown Flint. Deb and her husband were strong members of our church, very involved in women's and couple's ministry and as small group leaders.

But for Deb, news of my accident hit harder than most. Deb was a licensed emergency medical technician, and served as the supervisor in a dispatch office. Her company had not fielded the 911 call, but when Wendy called her private phone, Deb was sitting as usual at a bank of computer monitors, tracking their ambulances, taking calls and dispatching them to emergencies.

"John's been in an accident," Wendy said.

"Okay. Where?" was Deb's first response. She was unflappable in emergency situations.

"Lake Fenton. He was on a jet ski," Wendy said. "They had to pull him from the water."

I hope the person who found him was smart enough to get the water out of him, Deb thought clinically.

"And?" she asked.

"Um, he's not awake," Wendy said. "He's breathing but they've got a tube in him."

Deb's heart sank.

"How long do they think he was underwater?" Deb asked.

"Four or five minutes, ten minutes. They aren't sure," Wendy said.

"Okay," said Deb, her voice not betraying any of the deep

concern she now felt. They talked a bit more about a few details the doctors had supplied, and Deb jotted them down on a note pad.

"I wanted you to pray. That's why I'm calling everybody," Wendy said.

"Of course I will," Deb said. "Do you have people with you?"

"Yes, a lot of people came down to the hospital. It's good," said Wendy.

"Good," Deb affirmed. "I'll be praying from here until I see you. Call anytime you need me."

"Thank you, Deb," Wendy said.

As they hung up, Deb sighed heavily.

I'm glad Wendy doesn't have the perspective I have, because this is not looking good, Deb thought.

None of the elements of my situation added up to a good chance of survival. I had been hit on the head by a jet ski, been underwater five minutes or more. My heart had been re-started by a guy on scene. Now I was intubated.

Once you go on intubation, things get scary because there's a strong possibility you aren't coming off, she thought. *Once a machine is breathing for you, your chances go way down.*

She swiveled in her chair and looked away from her computer screens. Thankfully, it was a slow afternoon in their office. Her mind explored possibilities.

What will Wendy do if he doesn't make it? she wondered painfully. *I'll step in to help as much as I can. But she's going to need a lot of support.*

Deb had seen thousands of calls come in, and by sheer percentages, people in my condition rarely came back. She began to walk through the stages of my accident in her mind, as she imagined them happening, informed by her experience.

In Michigan, all drownings are considered cold water drownings, because the average water temperature never gets above sixty or seventy degrees. That means the body's responses are slower, giving EMTs more time to respond. When the body's responses are slower, people hold on longer to life.

Because I was floating in the cold water, my heart rate would have slowed, extending the use of oxygen in my bloodstream and especially to my brain. Blood would have been concentrated in my vital organs and core. As water came into my throat, laryngeal spasms would have kept that water from getting into my lungs for a time. Laryngeal spasms are the automatic reaction people have when a bit of water or food goes down the wrong pipe, causing constant coughing.

But after four or five minutes, those spasms stop and the lungs start to fill with water. The body relaxes. Water pours in. Oxygenation ceases.

A minute after that, brain damage starts. The brain craves oxygen, and uses an amazing eighteen percent of the blood in our bodies. Without oxygen, the brain simply starts to die. As wonderful as the brain is, it is also fragile.

In the rest of my body, the water in my lungs would have caused a cascade of events. There would have been a tremendous shift of fluid from inside my bloodstream and lungs to the space in between. Cells would have begun to die from lack of oxygen. My body would have swelled as these cells died and released their fluid.

He wasn't breathing. Somebody had to re-start his heart, she pondered. *Okay, what's the good news here?*

Deb imagined the paramedics arriving on scene. There

was an attitude among EMTs that said, "You're not going to die in my ambulance. You might die once I drop you off, but not in here." She knew that they would have worked on me every second I was in there.

She also knew that doctors never give someone a zero percent chance to live. As long as they are doing CPR, they won't admit total defeat. But two percent? When the chance was that low, it was in some measure an admission of defeat. They would already be thinking, *Is he donating his organs? Is he brain dead? Would the family even want him back in his condition?*

And then there was the intubation. Deb longed for details: When was I intubated? How long had I been intubated? Why? It was one thing to intubate someone right before surgery to keep them breathing during the procedure. That was more routine. But I had come in with lungs full of water, unconscious and with a probably oxygen-deprived brain. In these cases, where intubation was required to perform a function that a person's body was no longer performing on its own, the outlook was more dire.

Deb stepped away from the main control center and into her office. It had a sliding glass door and afforded little visual privacy, but she had never been bothered when others saw her pray. She knew that God could do anything, and He responded to prayer. She sat at her desk and leaned against her clasped hands.

Lord, even though I'm not at the hospital with others,
I join my prayers with theirs. You hear us wherever we
are, and so I ask you to save Pastor John. Save his life.
Go against the odds. Let the doctors be wrong. Give him
a miraculous recovery. You are well able and we receive
and stand on this promise of Pastor John's total healing
and recovery. Amen.

She leaned back in her chair. Her heart felt the feelings of
a year and a half earlier when Deb and her husband Brian
had been on the other side of an emergency situation with
their seventeen-year-old daughter, Kaitlyn. Kaitlyn's ma-
roon Pontiac Sunfire had hit a patch of ice, flipped three
times and landed on her. It was such a cold night that the
accident equipment kept freezing up. They didn't get her
body off the scene until midnight. John and Wendy came
to Deb and Brian's house that wintry, freezing night, to
console them.

It was Kaitlyn who had brought Deb and Brian to Mount
Hope Church Grand Blanc. She was dating a young man
who went there. "You should come to this church," Kaitlyn told her mom and dad. "The pastor is really funny."
So they had, and they stayed.

John performed Kaitlyn's funeral. He talked about her

love for showing horses, and he shared the gospel message, knowing that some people were there who might not hear it anywhere else. The service included times of praise and worship, and celebration that Kaitlyn was in her eternal home. Deb stood up, raised her arms and praised God. It never occurred to her to do anything else. That's what you had to do: praise him in all things. John and Wendy had helped teach her that.

Now she was the one extending a helping hand to Wendy and John in their time of great need.

"Lord, we're told we can have healing, and so we ask for it now," Deb prayed even as her co-workers and employees caught glances at her through the glass door. "Matthew 7:7 says to ask and keep on asking, knocking, seeking and receiving. I do that now, standing with John and Wendy. Be by his bedside now, healing and restoring him. Bring peace and comfort and strength to Wendy's heart now as she walks through this uncertainty."

CHAPTER 3

As if emerging from deep underwater, I came to semi-consciousness Saturday morning. I sensed people next to my bed, then heard the voices of a couple of close friends. I couldn't see them because my eyes felt heavy and hazy, but I recognized their voices.

"John, we're praying for you," said one. "You're going to be fine. You're going to make a full recovery. We believe God for that."

"Yes, the Lord's peace and restoration be with you," said the other. I nodded slightly to affirm and thank them. My eyes barely caught sight of a nurse in the room as well. On their way out, the visitors spoke a few words to her which I did not hear. Then they were gone. I fell back asleep.

A few hours later, I woke again, but this time was different. I found myself fully awake and thinking clearly. There was no sense of worry, only peace permeating my being — in spite of my obvious physical discomfort.

I must have really messed up on the jet ski, I thought to myself. I felt some large apparatus sticking down my throat, which did not feel good. Tubes were affixed to my arms, an IV machine and monitors. I couldn't move, and didn't really want to.

God, I don't know what happened, I prayed silently, *but here's an opportunity to believe You for healing. I don't know details. I just know I'm going to get better. I don't have one ounce of fear, worry or doubt that You will heal me. The devil may have given me his best shot, but he got beat again. I'm going to whip him by standing on your promises.*

I always try to approach life with a faith-filled attitude, seeing problems as opportunities to overcome, but in those moments my prayers felt super-charged. Little did I know that Wendy and so many were praying for me. By this time, less than eighteen hours after I crashed my XP Limited and went facedown in the lake, intercession was going up for me all over the world. Word had spread so fast. Even missionaries in other nations were praying and believing God for my recovery and healing. Had I known how the body of Christ in our region and beyond was rallying behind me, I would have been moved to tears.

But as Wendy drove to the hospital that morning, she had no idea in what condition she would find me. I had experienced lung failure, heart failure and possibly brain failure. *Would he be a vegetable?* she asked herself. *Was there brain damage? Would our lives ever be normal again?*

She took the elevator up to the fourth floor, and the nurses ushered her into my room. It was painted minty green and was just big enough for a bed, a bathroom, a small TV up in the corner, and a couple of chairs.

I was holding a clipboard on my bed and had already communicated with the nurses by writing on it, though my handwriting was terrible. Even under normal circumstances, people could barely read what I wrote. At the office they called it "Jo-lligraphy."

Wendy walked in and sat down. I could see the anxiety and questions all over her face, along with a quiet resolve, and a faith that obviously brought her peace. From her point of view, this was a defining moment in our lives.

He's awake — that's good news, she thought. *But what is his mind like?*

"Hey, John," she said. "How are you feeling?"

I didn't know it, but the question was loaded with meaning. I was just happy to see her. I took the clipboard in hand. First I scribbled the words, "Big wave."

Wendy nodded. *Okay, he has some faculties back. He remembers something. He can spell and write. It's pretty elementary, but so far so good.*

The next thing really caught her attention. I penned the words, "Michigan plays at 3:30."

If he remembers that his favorite team is playing today — he's definitely okay! Thank you, Lord! she thought. That answer alone lay to rest all her major concerns. *John's going to live, and he hasn't lost his mind!*

I wasn't done writing. I jotted a few last words: "It was worth it."

"Oh, my gosh," Wendy exclaimed in an "Are you kidding me?" tone. She shook her head. I smiled at her around my tube. There was nobody I would rather go through tough situations with than her.

Tori came in a little while later, face still puffy and tender. She was my football buddy in addition to my jet ski buddy, and we rarely missed a chance to watch the Wolverines destroy another team together. But first she burst into tears and hugged me as best she could around all my medical gear.

"I love you, Dad," she said. "I'm so glad you're okay."

I wrote with passion, "I love you, Tori. You are so special to me."

She grabbed the seat next to me and in spite of all our discomfort — Tori's teeth, and my whole body — we enjoyed every moment of the Michigan, Notre Dame game. Wendy came back in and saw us together, all beat up and cheering, and couldn't help thinking, *In the natural, this looks pretty pathetic, but in reality it's one of the most beautiful things I've seen in a long time.*

The nurses had given me a fairly strong vacuum tool called a suction straw, the kind they use at the dentist's office to suck extra saliva from your mouth when you can't swallow it. Whenever Michigan made a good play I banged that suction straw against the metal tray, filling the room with a metallic ringing tone. It sounded like victory.

"So many people are praying for you, Dad," Tori said at one point during the game. "In the waiting room, on Facebook, everywhere."

She paused and smiled, which made her wince a little. "I didn't know that many people knew you," she said. I smiled back and hit my suction straw a couple of times against the tray in approval.

Michigan beat Notre Dame that day. It was icing on the cake.

Still in the early stages of recovery, my body was doing everything it could to repair and remove excess fluid, so I tired easily. Upside down in the lake, my gastrointestinal track had pulled in probably a gallon and a half of water. My sinuses had filled up with around a pint of water, so my ears felt full. At one point our family physician, Dr. Boldman, came to check on me. He hefted a bottle holding my urine, which was streaming out via a catheter, and said to Wendy, "He's going to fill a lot of those."

Is this what I'm reduced to? I thought, knowing I was a passive participant as my body lay there and leaked all kinds of fluids. Then I changed my focus and thanked God that I was alive.

Life-Preserving Principle #6

When going through crisis, don't look at the circumstances.

Circumstances are fickle things — they can look dire one day and sunny the next.

Operating in faith according to God's Word tells us not to let what we see in the natural dictate our thoughts, words and actions, but instead what we see by our eyes of faith. One great man of faith said it like this: "I'm not moved by what I see. I'm not moved by what I feel. I'm moved only by what I believe."

Hebrews 11:1 agrees, reminding us that "faith is the substance of things hoped for, the evidence of things not seen." (NKJV) Elsewhere, the Bible says that "while we do not look at the things which are seen, but at the things which are not seen. For the things which are seen are temporary, but the things which are not seen are eternal." (2 Corinthians 4:18, NKJV)

So the things we see are only temporary and subject to change, but the things we do not see physically are real. Faith reaches out and lays hold of those things that Jesus provided for us in the atonement. Faith looks beyond the natural and sees the finished work or healing.

It's very important to see yourself living out the promises of God you are claiming for yourself. You have to see it on the inside before it happens on the outside. The Bible calls this faith, and with it we not only receive the promises, but we please God.

Much of the liquid I was eliminating came from the IV fluids the hospital gave me to keep my blood pressure up. My lungs were traumatized and had the same kind of problem that premature infants have: a lack of surfactant, a complex mixture of lipids, proteins and carbohydrates critical to breathing function. My body was trying to re-manufacture it at a desperate pace.

That's why, when Wendy stepped into the hall with the doctors to look over their shoulders at the X-rays that day, she saw something strange: a field of white where my lungs should have been. The doctors nodded soberly.

It's like John's lungs aren't even there, she thought. *Now we know how to specifically pray.*

Word spread quickly through Wendy's reports that I had awakened and was thinking normally. That was a great encouragement to the people in the church. One of them reminded us that for six weeks before the accident, I had preached a series on the names of God. Each week was a new name and a new promise represented by the name of God. People began recalling those Bible promises through the names of God — how he rescues, provides, supplies, and so much more — and prayed them for my situation. "All those Bible promises were fresh and brand new for us," one member said. "Somehow, God and Pastor John prepared us for this."

Word also got around about the funny things I wrote

on the board and how I was encouraging the staff at the hospital, even though I couldn't yet speak because of the tube. I found the nurses so encouraging that I couldn't help but give back to them. I especially enjoyed talking about the Lord and how life was so much better with him in control. It seemed to me that they were listening with more than just polite attention.

One person we chose not to tell about the accident was my mom, because she had dementia and might not have understood. But my sister Diana and her husband Randy drove over from Grand Rapids, came into the room, grabbed my hand, hugged me and prayed for me passionately. It was a special visit from the person who had first led me to the Lord.

On Sunday morning, a day after I had woken up, my oldest daughter, Julia, arrived after a marathon drive from Arizona. Upon getting the call from Wendy, she had thrown her stuff into the car and driven non-stop with Jim, her Beta fish in a cup, pulling over only to fill up with gas. She walked in my room and stood by my bedside.

Oh my gosh, she thought. *He looks twice his size!*

She glanced at Wendy. Wendy nodded and gave her a look like, "It's real."

I tried to smile as she glanced me over. I was amazed to see her there and wished I could greet her with words and a big embrace, but I had to write my thoughts down instead. Of all my kids, Julia is the most like me: high-achieving, organized, driven and capable of drawing others to pursue the same goal. When she was attending our church, half the youth group was there because of her.

She pulled up a chair and talked to me for a while. She looked weary from the drive but also relieved that her dad was communicating with her, and that Wendy and I were relaxed and peaceful about the whole thing. Julia had been planning to come home for a week of vacation that month anyway. She soon decided to stay for a month to help out the family in a way that really impressed and gratified me. There were phone calls to be made, emails to be written, people to be rallied, and home life to be maintained with the other kids. She stepped up and was a crucial source of strength to Wendy. Julia helped anchor our family in those days after the accident.

Another major help was Ted Milian, my right-hand man at the church. Ted was a former offensive lineman for the Edmonton Eskimos in the Canadian Football League. He won a number of Grey Cups with the team. We often had lunch together during the workweek. I had noticed that when Ted got a bag of potato chips with his meal, he always opened the bag up completely so it was flat, and ate the chips from a pile. I finally asked him one day, "Why do you do that? Why don't you stick your hand in the bag and grab chips from there?" He held the chips bag up next to his open hand and said, "Can you figure it out now?" I realized then that his hand was simply too big to fit inside.

Ted was a gifted COO who ran the business of the ministry and had a natural sense of how to lead people through crisis. He knew that if the leaders freaked out, the people would freak out. He also walked in strong faith and stood on the promises of God, so I was happy to have him in charge.

Still, his reaction upon first seeing me was like the others.

It looks like someone took a broken baseball bat and worked him over, he thought, staring at my swollen face and busted teeth. *He's almost unrecognizable — disfigured, larger. If you pricked him with a pin I bet he'd ooze liquid for an hour.*

I was glad there were no mirrors handy, given the way Ted and the others were staring at me. But I knew Ted was a fighter, like I was, and would stand with us all the way.

"Hey, John," he said, moving toward my bed. "You know,

there are easier ways to get testimonies than to smash your body on a jet ski."

I chuckled in spite of the pain it caused in my throat. Ted often acted as a foil to my driven, focused personality. He joked with me in front of the other staff, which helped people to relax, and helped me not to take myself too seriously.

We discussed a few key things that needed to be done in my absence. Ted was already filling the Sundays ahead with speakers, calling people connected with our ministry to give them personal updates, and keeping the church steady by communicating well and encouraging everyone to continue praying for the miracle of my recovery.

Before he left, I asked for one more thing. I wrote the request on the board: "Bring in a bunch of healing promises from God's word and put them on the wall." Ted read it and nodded "Okay." I had many of God's scriptural promises memorized, but I wanted to be surrounded by them, to meditate on them and let them sink into my heart. At that point I had not yet heard the word that Harry and Cheryl Salem had received about my recovery — though I was certainly living it.

Life-Preserving Principle #7

When going through a crisis, keep God's promises before your eyes, in your mouth and in your ears.

I learned early on in my walk with God that the crisis of life comes to us all. Jesus said in John 16:33, "These things I have spoken to you, that in Me you may have peace. In the world you will have tribulation; but be of good cheer, I have overcome the world." (NKJV)

As long as we are alive on this planet, we will probably have something trying to affect us in a negative way. It's important to understand that as Christians, we have been redeemed from the curse and it is our responsibility to enforce Christ's victory in our personal lives. Jesus was crucified on a cross and took upon Himself the sin of all mankind, and He also took all of our diseases and sicknesses. The gospel of Matthew 8:17 says Jesus healed people "that it might be fulfilled which was spoken by Isaiah the prophet, saying: 'He Himself took our infirmities, and bore our sicknesses.'" (NKJV)

"Took" or "bore" in the Greek means "to bear or lift with the idea of total removal." Faith reaches out and lays hold of the promises of God. Remember, regardless of the crisis or the trial or the sickness or the attack or the problem, there is absolutely nothing that God can't heal or rescue you from.

The Psalmist penned these words: "I will bless the Lord at all times; His praise shall continually be in my mouth." (34:1, NKJV) Notice the words "at all times" — when things are going well and when things are not going well. He went on to write, "Oh, magnify the Lord with me, and let us exalt His name together." (34:3, NKJV)

In every situation we have a choice to magnify our problems or magnify the Lord and His promises. In other words: we are to talk the solution and the promises of God over our circumstances, and not talk the problem. The Bible tells us that God inhabits the praises of His people. When the Lord enters the situation, freedom always follows.

Psalms 34:4 goes on to say:
I sought the Lord, and He heard me,
And delivered me from all my fears.
As we seek the Lord, He delivers us from "all fears." Regardless of the circumstances in your life, God is bigger and greater than all of them. The psalmist ended with these words:
The righteous cry out, and the Lord hears,
And delivers them out of all their troubles.
Many are the afflictions of the righteous,

But the Lord delivers him out of them all. (34:17, 19)

Even though we encounter trouble in the world, the Lord will deliver us out of them all. Our part is to believe and apply God's Word in every situation, and then expect the freedom, the breakthrough, the healing we desire.

Ted went back to the office and enlisted Eric, our worship leader and graphic designer, to select healing promises from the Bible and print ten or twelve of them on big, colorful legal-size paper. Ted brought them in the next day and taped them to the walls all around my room. Each scripture was a source of comfort and confidence, but one absolutely captivated my attention. Jeremiah 30:17 read, "'For I will restore health to you and heal you of your wounds,' says the Lord".

I stared at that verse as if my eyes were glued to it.

I will restore health to you and heal you of your wounds. It was like God himself was speaking to me. I repeated it over and over in my mind, and literally felt faith and healing spread throughout my body. I now had a specific, living "now" promise from God for me, and I never got tired of repeating it in my mind. *I will restore health to you and heal you of your wounds.*

Yes, Lord! my heart shouted.

Joy bubbled up in me, and I was laughing on the inside knowing that this was the truth about my situation, not the daily doctors' reports or even my own feelings. The facts boomed inside my soul: God would restore health to me and heal all of my wounds. Period. Nothing else could touch that. Once you hear from heaven, you know the final score, even if there's time left in the game. Jeremiah 30:17 became my battle cry.

That battle cry was tested every morning at about 7:30 when the doctors gathered outside my room to discuss my recovery. I could look to my left through the ICU window and see them meeting: my cardiologist, Dr. Boldman, several other specialists — and Wendy.

The first time Wendy walked up and stood with them, the doctors looked at her as if to ask, "What are you doing here?"

"I'm his wife," Wendy said. "I want to see the X-rays and hear what you have to say."

They looked at each other, a little miffed at her presence, but unable to tell her to leave. The pulmonary specialist pulled out the X-rays. My lungs were still white.

"Just like before," the specialist said. "No change."

Well, more work to do in prayer, Wendy thought. *God, I know you will clear them up.*

"We want to keep him intubated," said Dr. Boldman. "He seems to be responding well, even though I'm concerned about those lungs."

I knew the doctors were having a tough time squaring the evidence on the X-rays of severely damaged lungs with the cheerful, increasingly-healthy-looking man in the room.

"We'll know more tomorrow," Boldman concluded, and the meeting disbanded. Wendy immediately sent word to friends and supporters: "John's attitude and recovery are going great, but we need to keep praying for his lungs. The X-rays are white, white, white."

The next day she joined their circle again. The new X-rays came: white. Nothing showed progress in my lungs.

"Hm," said Dr. Boldman, then glanced at me in my room. He and the other doctors seemed baffled. I was totally alert and had already had some fun "conversations" with the nurses via my white board. I usually asked them how their shift was going and thanked them for all they were doing. One decision that made this possible was my refusal to have any sedatives, which would have rendered me less aware of the pain of the tube in my throat, but also less alert and sharp. I wanted to be in control of my faculties, to be having a real experience and real conversations during my time there.

Dr. Boldman seemed to be wondering how a guy with lungs like mine could be behaving like I was.

"Let's see where we're at tomorrow," he said.

The next morning, too, Wendy expected the X-rays to be clear, but they were white again.

More work to do in prayer, she thought. On some days, she walked the beautiful nature trails surrounding the medical center and prayed for my healing before even coming in. By the time of the doctors' powwow, her faith felt rock solid.

Finally, on day four, the X-rays caught up with the facts. Even Wendy could see dark places where the lungs were stabilizing and returning to normal function.

"Improvement," said the pulmonary specialist as the other doctors nodded. Doctors aren't the celebrating type, and Dr. Boldman in particular was reserved and somewhat stoic, though gentle and very professional.

"Good," he said. "Progress."

That seemed like an understatement. I knew my body was healing very rapidly, and that could only happen supernaturally. Wendy got the message out, "His lungs showed up on the X-rays today! Good news. They're healing!"

The next time Ted walked in, he stopped for a moment and took a long look at me. His expression was different than before.

"You're getting better," he said. "For the first time, I can see it."

I nodded. It was one thing to trust God in spite of the evidence; it was another to see a miracle manifest before your very eyes. I smiled, feeling like a living miracle.

"By the way," he said, "Wendy's doing very, very well. People believe in her. She's tough. She comes across as easy-going, but she has guts. She's doing a great job."

"Thank you," I wrote. "I agree 100%."

On day three, another encouragement arrived from Lansing where so many of our friends were. A trusted intercessor sent word that she had heard from the Lord that I would experience complete healing. That brought a lot of comfort and confirmation to our whole family. With that and many other encouraging words and promises, we soldiered forward.

My next goal was to get my lungs functioning on their own — and get rid of that painful breathing tube. The nurses started by reducing the amount of oxygen I was receiving, and I responded well, for the most part. But when they pulled the tube out that first time, my oxygen level fell so much that they had to put it in again. Not only that, but my lungs were showing signs of pneumonia.

There's no victory without a fight, I thought.

But these events were like blips along a predetermined road leading to full, fast recovery. Within a day or so I was so strong that the nurses began talking about removing the tube again.

"Tomorrow's the day," a nurse informed me. "You're going to have to learn to eat again."

"That shouldn't be hard," I wrote.

She smiled and stopped to chat a moment.

"You know, your recovery is becoming legendary," she

said. "What blows us away is your attitude. Nobody acts like this when they came as close to death as you did."

I nodded.

"Thank you," I wrote. "I'm glad to hear it. Everybody's help is making a big difference."

I realized how encouraging it is for medical professionals to witness an amazing recovery, especially when a patient is given a two percent chance to live. God doesn't just deliver victory to one person, but to everyone around that person. So it was a huge win for the RNs and I'm sure it raised their hope level for a long time after that. I can only imagine how many other patients benefited from the staff's elevated level of hope because of how God was pulling me back from the brink of death.

On the evening of the fourth day, the nurses ever-so-slowly pulled the tube out. I felt it scraping against the inside of my throat, and it felt like it just kept coming. I was surprised how far down it had gone. Then the whole thing emerged — a corrugated, plastic tube. Massive relief settled onto my chest.

No wonder it felt so uncomfortable, I thought, looking at that beast. I had my throat back now.

As expected, I kept coughing up the junk accumulating in my lungs, so the suction device came in handy. My mouth and lips were swollen and scarred up. A plastic surgeon had already repaired my lip and there were stitches down my chin and mouth. My clavicle was still achy and bruised.

After an hour they gave me some Jell-O. It slid down my throat. Pretty quickly, my muscles reacted and began swallowing food as eagerly as I felt.

For the first time since Friday, I could talk — slowly and briefly, but it was quite a relief to express myself with spoken words instead of notes on a board. The first thing I did was begin reading those scriptures out loud, frequently. I was like a machine gun confessing the promises of God. I opened the Bible and read it as well.

"Lord, I thank you that according to Jesus Christ I am healed. That at the cross you provided and paid for my healing. That you rescued and redeemed me." On and on I went, feeling strength restored to me even as I spoke. My favorite was still from Jeremiah: "Lord, you will heal my body and restore my health completely!"

What a gift it was to be able to talk and to sit up in bed. Walking, however, was surprisingly shaky at first. When I took my first steps I actually felt my legs tremble underneath me.

What in the world? I thought. I was unaware how quickly basic life skills are lost.

"Whoa, take it very easy. Take it very easy," the nurse said. "Your attitude is great, but your body needs time to catch up."

This nurse was a man and had the strength to help me with those first unsteady steps. My legs were sore, too, having been bruised and banged up in the accident itself. I made a point to get up every hour so my legs would get stronger.

The day they pulled the tube out I was resting and sitting up in bed, enjoying my newfound "freedom" when I opened my eyes from a catnap and saw the superintendent of our church's district, Bill Leach.. I was amazed. Bill was responsible for overseeing hundreds of churches in Michigan, and he had taken time to drive over from his office a couple of hours away to visit me personally. We enjoyed a meaningful time of conversation and prayer. When they left, Bill told me, "John, God's healing you up. It's incredible what's happening. Use this time to listen to God. Let him give you direction — and just heal up and rest."

It was great advice.

***

I was getting better by the hour. On Thursday, they transferred me out of the ICU and into a regular room. That evening they told me I was ready to go home, if I wanted — and I very much did. My X-rays were looking better every time. The pneumonia had not gone away completely, but my oxygen levels were great. I was still only around eighty-five percent healed, but I could finish my recovery at home.

Dr. Boldman came in for a final visit.

"John, how are you feeling?" he asked.

"Really good, considering," I said. I was still coughing frequently, and my face and parts of my body felt bruised. But overall I felt healthy again.

"My chest still hurts a little bit," I mentioned.

"That's because the guy punched you a few hundred times," Dr. Boldman said.

That makes sense, I thought, feeling the tender area where Brian's fist had pounded me — and brought me back to life. My clavicle, too, was broken, but the doctors had recommended against surgery because they were confident it would heal on its own.

After our chat, Dr. Boldman stopped and leaned against the door of my room, staring at me. Then he began shaking his head. It was unusual behavior for him.

"What?" I finally asked, feeling disconcerted.

"We hardly ever, ever see anything like this," he said. "With what happened to you, and the recovery rate you're on. You were so mangled, beat-up and abused in this accident. But you've had a complete turnaround. Here you are leaving the hospital seven days later. We hardly ever see that."

With that, he smiled and walked out, still shaking his head. To hear those words from such a well-known, unflappable professional surprised even me. In all our years going to Dr. Boldman for problems big and small, I had never seen him display such surprise and even emotion.

Of course, I had never walked through a miracle like this before. It was an inspiring thing to know in my heart what would happen, and see it unfold in real time. So many human opinions had been proven wrong in the process. I wasn't brain dead. I had no lingering lung or heart problems. My mental state was just like it was before. And now I was going home.

On a sunny September afternoon, one week after the accident, hospital orderlies wheeled me in a wheelchair to our car. I could have walked, but I thought I may as well take advantage of the rest. They closed the passenger door behind me. Wendy sat in the driver's seat, smiling and ready to go.

"Hey," I said.

"Hey," she said. "I love you."

"I love you, too," I said. "I'm ready to go home."

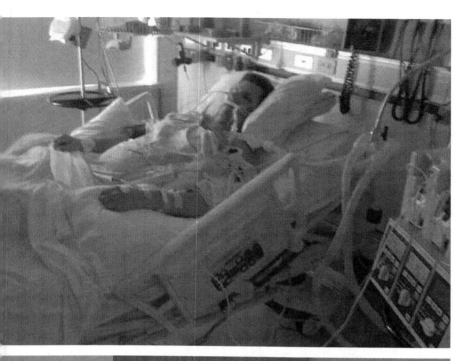

But He was wounded for
our transgressions, He was
bruised for our iniquities;
the chastisement for our peace
was upon Him, and by His

Acts 10:38
how God anointed
of Nazareth with th
and with power, w
ood and he
ppressed by
e was with H

For I will restore
health to you and
heal you of your
wounds, says the
Lord.
Jeremiah 30:17

in His own b
that we, ha
might live f
by whose st
healed.
l Peter 2:24

to Jerusalem, bringing sick peopl
clean spirits, and they

Luke 10:8-10
Whatever city yo
and they receive
such things as a
you. And heal th

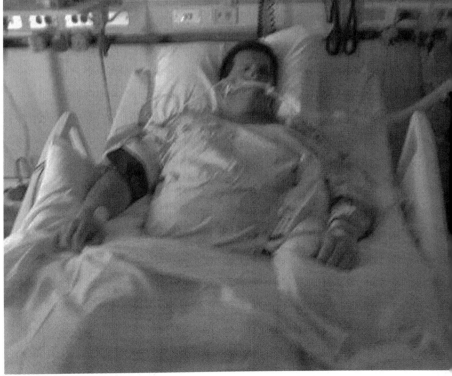

CHAPTER 4

Instead of praying me back from the brink, now the
people of the church and community were rejoicing that
I was mostly well. Our team of staff and volunteers was
strong and empowered to carry out their ministries, so
they had kept everything running smoothly. It eased my
mind to know that the church was in good hands. Everything that normally happened — outstanding worship,
missions teams preparing to go around the world, awesome children's ministry and everything else — kept happening at the same high level. I was proud of them.

Of course, when I came back they acted like they needed
me, but that's just because they loved me.

When Ted heard I was out of the hospital, he was completely stunned.

"This was a supernatural recovery, plain and simple," he
declared to the staff. "He came in to the hospital looking
like toast, from a human point of view. It was the Lord

who brought him through and healed him."

Ted then began fighting a barely disguised battle to keep me home for a while, to fully rest and recover. He knew my "gotta do" list would grow. Somehow they were able to keep me off the church premises until October.

For Deb Tangen, the EMT supervisor, my recovery was especially meaningful. More than most people, she knew what I was up against — and what the stakes were in losing a loved one. When Ted told the congregation how I was fighting for my miracle by having the healing scriptures posted around my room, Deb got chills.

Talk about walking out your faith, she thought. *Here's a man doing all the things he preaches — standing on the Word, speaking the promises, not letting circumstances dictate reality. He's putting all those principles into practice.*

It gave her and her husband comfort knowing that they had been part of our miracle through prayer.

One guy I hadn't seen since the accident was Brian, the one who pulled me from the lake. At my request, he dropped by the church office. Appreciation and love welled up in me as I saw him. I gave him a big hug.

"You've got to know that God used you," I told him. "There was nobody else on the lake, or they were so far from the accident that they didn't see me. If you hadn't turned around and looked, this story would have ended in tragedy."

He seemed uncomfortable with the praise, but it was well-earned.

"Thank you for rescuing me," I said. "Because of you I'm here."
"I was just doing what I knew to do," he said.

Wendy came in and shook his hand warmly.

"Thank you so much for what you did," she reiterated. "Because of you and the way God used your efforts, I have my husband and my kids have their father."

Until Wendy had called him a few days after the accident, he didn't even know if I had survived.

"All I did was what anyone else would do," Brian said, blushing. "If I crashed I hope someone would be there."

For weeks after that, I texted and called Brian frequently to thank him and offer him a steak dinner anytime we got together. For Brian's part, his intersection with my life came at a key time. He had assumed I was a random guy out partying and drinking on the lake. When he learned I was a pastor, he considered it a revelation and an open door to a new path in his own life.

Here I am chasing money and pleasure, and yet I'm the one who rescued this man of God from death, he thought. He couldn't make sense of it, but he knew God was speaking through it and telling him to get back on track.

At home, I felt well, but my body was still healing. Among other things, my teeth and gums were chipped up and damaged. My left clavicle was still mending, as were my legs, chest, lungs and so on. Doctors gave me an oxygen tank and mask and told me to use it, even though I felt good. I obeyed their orders, and with their permission began to get up and move around more and more each day. When resting, I lay there quietly and listened to what the Lord was speaking to my heart.

A doctor friend of ours, Dr. Bouvier, looked at my medical records soon after the accident, and his conclusion was pretty sobering:

"Your prognosis was grave," he told me. "You were not expected to live. Probably two percent or less. The main problem was that you had heart failure. Water had filled your lungs, and they were certainly worried that your brain was compromised because you were down some-where between six to twelve minutes. Anything over four minutes, we consider that person probably to be brain dead."

He shook his head and looked at me with gratitude.

"When the prognosis is grave and as poor as it was, and you call the family, it's kind of a prep for the inevitable," he informed me. "Having the heart stop, and the lungs stop, and the brain function stop, and then come back to life again — that's the miracle. That just doesn't happen."

Dr. Bouvier was a strong Christian and a highly experi-enced medical doctor with tens of thousands of hours in the ER. He paused for a moment, seeming to compare my experience with his extensive background in the field.

"Circumstances can align themselves so perfectly that an outcome happens that you know it was God," he said, nodding his head and smiling. "It was God that hap-pened."

When he left, I pondered the fact that though I had lost consciousness and technically died for a period of time, I didn't see heaven, didn't experience a tunnel of light, didn't meet long lost relatives or anything like that. If I had, it would have made the recovery a lot harder. God knows my personality. If I had seen him face to face, I never would have wanted to come back. I like to keep moving forward, and I'm certain that the glorious joys of heaven and his presence would have been too much for me to leave. Still, God is the author of life, not death, and in his sovereignty it was not my time to go. I am determined never to go before my time but to enjoy life as a precious gift and use whatever I have to serve God and people.

One evening we were sitting around the table after dinner and Wendy looked at me sort of strangely.

"What is it?" I finally asked.

"When people ask about you, I almost don't know what to say," she said. "You're doing so well. To go from almost drowning, to a week later you're out of the hospital breathing on your own — it's just amazing. It happened so fast."

We meditated again on the powerful work of God in our lives and in that situation. For my part, I felt galvanized in my calling again. God had not let me die, therefore there was more work to do. I was ready and excited.

On October 18, five weeks after the accident, our church held a big victory service. Doctors and paramedics joined me on stage, as did my XP Limited, to give people a visual of what had happened. Brian was there, and Ted played the host and interviewer. The place was packed.

The biggest impact on the audience came when doctors talked about how serious my condition had been when I arrived at the hospital. A hush came over everyone as they understood the reality of how close I was to dying.

Brian shared, too, and that day he told me that he had dedicated his life to the Lord.

I spoke as well, and my message to the people was simple.

"I'm sorry for putting you through this," I said first. "It was my fault, not anyone else's and not some sort of punishment. I don't have sin in my life that God was trying to correct. I was just over-zealous in hitting that big wake. God didn't do it — I did. People often wrongly think God is putting them through a bad circumstance. On the contrary, He's working for your good even when the thief tries to steal, kill and destroy. It is God's nature to heal and restore, and that's what happened to me."

I continued, "On the other hand, some people say that if you're living right, accidents like this won't happen. But Jesus said clearly in John 16, in this world we will have trouble, but take heart, for he has overcome this world. I see this not as a curse but an opportunity to live by the faith we express. Then it becomes an actual blessing to those around us who marvel at God's grace at work in our lives. My message to all of us is, 'Look what the Lord has done. There are still things to accomplish, people to reach with the gospel, disciples to cultivate, a region and area to impact, and a great God to worship. We've got a lot of stuff to do!'"

People erupted in praise.

Life-Preserving Principle #8

When going through a crisis, remember who is the Author of life and who is the villain in your story.

If your life is a story written as you live each day, then it's important to keep the characters straight. Every good story has heroes, villains and a battle to fight. In the battle for your life and mine, the hero and rescuer is Jesus. The devil, or Satan, that old dragon, is the villain. Jesus put it like this: "The thief comes only in order to steal and kill and destroy. I came that they may have and enjoy life, and have it in abundance [to the full, till it overflows]." (John 10:10, AMP) Another translation says it like this: "The thief's purpose is to steal and kill and destroy. My purpose is to give them a rich and satisfying life." (NLT) After God rescued and healed me from my jet ski accident, people would ask me, "Why do you think this happened? Was there sin in your life? Did you do something wrong?" Thankfully, I can say, "No." I start most days in prayer. One of my prayers is, "God if there is anything displeasing I am doing, in thought, word, or action, please reveal it to me and I'll change it immediately." Am I perfect? No. But my accident was not God punishing me for some sin of which I wasn't even aware.

The thing I did wrong? I was too zealous with speed. I took those awesome waves Brian created with his boat. I did not let go in time, and gravity smacked me upside the head.

Was that God's will? No. Keep the hero and the villain straight. It's the thief that comes to steal, kill, and destroy and Jesus who brings life with abundance. That's exactly what He did for me!

In the days that followed, I lived with a growing sense of awe and amazement. A renewed sense of vision came upon me — the same vision that God had put on our hearts two decades earlier: to reach all of Grand Blanc, Genesee County and the world with the life-changing gospel message of Jesus Christ.

Of course, some people had unexpected reactions when they first saw me. The lady who cuts my hair immediately started crying when I walked into her salon. Then she hit me!

"What are you doing?" I asked her.
"I don't know whether to hit you again or to hug you!" she said.

"But I'm alive and completely healed," I protested.

"I don't care!" she said. That's when I began to see how deeply connected each of us is to others around us, and how our behavior touches everyone. All I could do was apologize again for doing something stupid.

Back in the church office, I was meeting with a staff member to go over logistics one day. During our conversation I caught her looking at me sideways.

"What's going on?" I asked.

She responded, "It's like this isn't even real. You almost died and here you are in front of me. I can't help wondering, is this real? Am I talking to this guy?"

Reactions like that were humbling for me, and again made me excited to be back doing what God had given me to do.

I was still seeing the doctors, driving myself to appointments. The lung specialist would mostly just look at my X-rays and shake his head. After a month he said, "You've got a clean bill of health. You're completely well. You don't have to see me again." We shook hands and I left, gratefully. I still jog regularly on the nature path around Genesys, and when I see the ICU room windows I pray for the people there. I have been one of them.

Wendy and I agreed I should get back on the jet ski soon. There was no sense letting it become a stronghold of fear. When spring warmed up the lake, we took the jet skis out. It took some mental strength to overcome my own resistance to ride again, but I took it slow and built back up little by little. After three or four outings I was mostly back to normal. I whipped around and went as fast as I could, but when I got behind a boat and saw a deep wake, I didn't hit it as hard. Every time I jumped and got air, I was more reserved and wiser about it. I also taught myself how to go over wakes: one foot back, one foot forward, to hold the jet ski steady against the kick of hitting the wake.

And I became a strong advocate for wearing proper life vests — ones that actually keep your head out of water when you lose consciousness.

***

One of the big results of the situation was how much more I appreciated my natural and spiritual families — and I had loved them with all my heart before the accident. Wendy in particular impressed me so much with her faith and ability to lead people through a tough circumstance. Sometimes it takes a crisis to reveal the full amount of strength in people. I realized anew what a priceless gift each person in my life is.

Wendy had taught swim lessons at our local fitness center in exchange for membership for years. Every two years the instructors had to renew their CPR training. The first time she went to a CPR class after my accident, she unexpectedly began tearing up during the demonstration.

That was John, she thought as the instructor pushed on the mannequin's chest. It seemed so clinical in this setting compared to the actual scene of my accident. Finally, Wendy raised her hand and cleared her throat which was clenched with emotion.

"I know we're asking a lot of questions like, 'How long do you stay with it?' and, 'What are the best techniques?'" she said. "I want you to know that my husband John was in an accident. The guy who rescued him didn't have good circumstances. He couldn't lay John out on the ground because they were in the water. And he barely had any technique because he was floating. He had to beat on his chest repeatedly, and pretty hard. Because he did that, and didn't give up, my husband is here."

She paused as a wave of feeling washed over her.

"You don't have to have perfect circumstances," she continued. "Just do something. I know we're here to get our certificates so we can continue teaching swim lessons and other things. But these skills really do make a difference. You can actually save a life with this. And you never know when it'll happen. So if you find yourself doing this in real life, don't give up in frustration at your lack of technique or bad circumstances or apparent failure. Do whatever you can — and keep doing it."

Those words, "Do what you can, and keep doing it," seemed to sum up the best lessons of my accident, and of our lives. Having miraculously survived, I was going to keep doing what God made me to do, even through times of frustration or adverse circumstances. Wendy felt the same way. We would pour out our lives and energy to fulfill the callings He has so graciously given us.

How could we do otherwise? *For He restored health to me and healed all my wounds.*

HOW DO I KNOW?

How does a person really know where they go after death? The Bible is so clear on this. Heaven is real, Hell is real and eternity is real, and what you do with the person of Jesus Christ will determine your outcome. God loves you and he wants to give you the gift and the assurance of eternal life. The Bible tells us – whoever calls on the name of the Lord will be saved. Say this prayer right now: Dear Lord, Right now I repent of all my sin, forgive me for breaking your laws and commands. I boldly confess Jesus Christ as my Savior and Lord. I choose to live for you all the days of my life. Thank you Lord for granting me the gift of eternal life. Amen.

"For God so loved the world that He gave His only begotten Son, that whoever believes in Him should not perish but have everlasting life." John 3:16

Romans 10 verses 9 and 13 says that "if you confess with your mouth the Lord Jesus and believe in your heart that God has raised Him from the dead, you will be saved. … For 'whoever calls on the name of the Lord shall be saved.'"

Contact Information for Pastor John Galinetti and his book, 2% Chance to Live

Pastor John Galinetti
8363 Embury Rd.
Grand Blanc, MI 48439

Email to: 2percent@mhcgb.com

Additional information available at:

Address: **Mount Hope Church**

8363 Embury Rd.

Grand Blanc, MI 48439

Email: **info@mhcgb.com**

Phone :   **810 695-0461**

Fax: **810-695-7466**

Website: **www.mhcgb.com**

Facebook: **https://www.facebook.com/mhcgb/**

Twitter: **@MountHope_Grand Blanc**

Instagram: **mhcgb**

SEE PASTOR JOHN GALINETTI SHARE HIS STORY "FROM TRAGEDY TO TRIUMPH" IN PERSON. ORDER A COPY OF THE DVD TODAY!!

You can order directly from the Mount Hope Church website at www.mhcgb.com

LEARN HOW TO EXERCISE THE FAITH YOU ALREADY POSSESS
IN JOHN GALINETTI'S FIRST BOOK, PROGRESSIONS OF FAITH.
ORDER AT MHCGB.COM

PROGRESSIONS OF
FAITH

Succeeding
in Life's
Faith
Journey

John Galinetti

ABOUT JOHN GALINETTI

John Galinetti is the founding pastor of Mount Hope
Church, a growing church in Grand Blanc, Michigan.
He and his wife Wendy started the church in 1988.
Relentlessly, Pastor John has dedicated himself to help
people maximize their personal and spiritual potential for
the cause of Christ.

Pastor John is heard daily on popular radio stations. His
upbeat and motivating program called "The Pastor's
Minute" reaches more than 60,000 commuters and offices
who make it a regular part of their work day throughout
Michigan.

The miraculous recovery from of a fatal jet ski accident
in 2009 has not slowed his pace or motivation. His
passion and drive is evident as he continues to fervently
preach the gospel in 18 nations including cultural centers,
packed-out stadiums and sporting arenas.

Pastor John holds credentials with the Michigan District
of the Assemblies of God and is a graduate of Global
University and Rhema Bible Training Center. He has
authored two books, Progressions Of Faith and 2%
Chance To Live. He has also been featured on the 700
Club television program.

Pastor John is an avid Michigan football fan,
outdoorsman, and loves spending time with Wendy and
their four children.